MATH Expressions
Common Core

Dr. Karen C. Fuson

GRADE

1

Volume 1

This material is based upon work supported by the
National Science Foundation
under Grant Numbers
ESI-9816320, REC-9806020, and RED-935373.

Any opinions, findings, and conclusions, or recommendations expressed in this material
are those of the author and do not necessarily reflect the views of the National Science Foundation.

VOLUME 1 CONTENTS

UNIT 1 Partners and Number Patterns Through 10

© Houghton Mifflin Harcourt Publishing Company

VOLUME 1 CONTENTS *(continued)*

 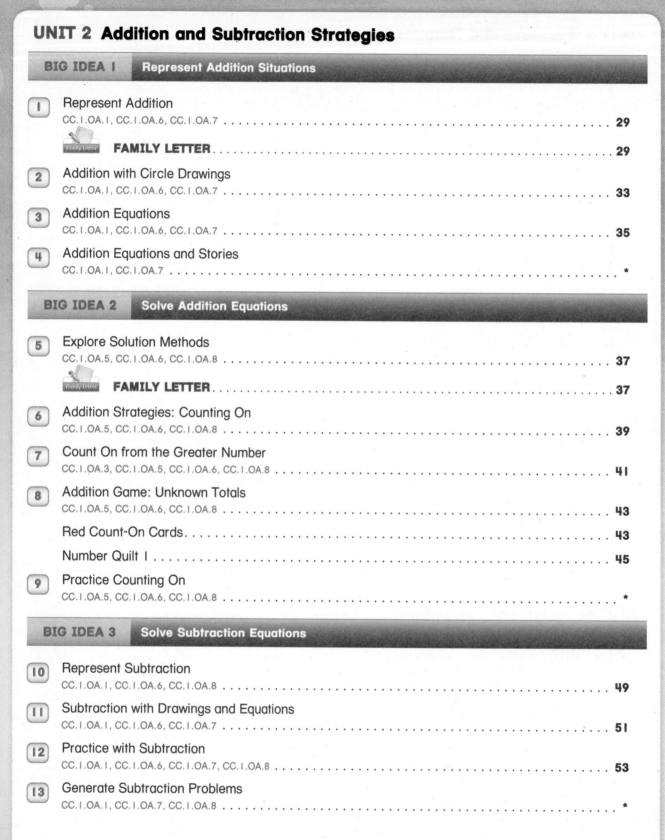
© Houghton Mifflin Harcourt Publishing Company

* This lesson consists only of activities from the Teacher Edition.

UNIT 3 Unknown Numbers in Addition and Subtraction

© Houghton Mifflin Harcourt Publishing Company

* This lesson consists only of activities from the Teacher Edition.

UNIT 4 Place Value Concepts

© Houghton Mifflin Harcourt Publishing Company

* This lesson consists only of activities from the Teacher Edition.

© Houghton Mifflin Harcourt Publishing Company

* This lesson consists only of activities from the Teacher Edition.

Family Letter

Dear Family:

Your child is learning math in an innovative program that interweaves abstract mathematical concepts with the everyday experiences of children. This helps children to understand math better.

In this program, your child will learn math and have fun by:

- working with objects and making drawings of math situations;
- working with other children and sharing problem solving strategies with them;
- writing and solving problems and connecting math to daily life;
- helping classmates learn.

Your child will have homework almost every day. He or she needs a **Homework Helper.** The helper may be anyone—you, an older brother or sister (or other family member), a neighbor, or a friend. Make a specific time for homework and provide your child with a quiet place to work (for example, no TV). Encourage your child to talk about what is happening in math class. If your child is having problems with math, please talk to me to see how you might help.

Thank you. You are vital to your child's learning.

Sincerely,
Your child's teacher

COMMON CORE Unit 1 includes the Common Core Standards for Mathematical Content for Operations and Algebraic Thinking 1.OA.1, 1.OA.3, 1.OA.5, 1.OA.6, 1.OA.8 and all Mathematical Practices.

- -

Please fill out the following information and return this form to the teacher.

My child _____ will have _____
               (child's name)   (Homework Helper's name)

as his or her Homework Helper. This person is my

child's _____.
          (relationship to child)

Carta a la familia

Estimada familia:

Su niño está aprendiendo matemáticas con un programa innovador que relaciona conceptos matemáticos abstractos con la experiencia diaria de los niños. Esto ayuda a los niños a entender mejor las matemáticas.

Con este programa, su niño aprenderá matemáticas y se divertirá mientras:

- trabaja con objetos y hace dibujos de problemas matemáticos;
- trabaja con otros niños y comparte estrategias para resolver problemas;
- escribe y resuelve problemas y relaciona las matemáticas con la vida diaria;
- ayuda a sus compañeros a aprender.

Su niño tendrá tarea casi todos los días y necesita a una persona que lo ayude con la tarea. Esa persona puede ser usted, un hermano mayor (u otro familiar), un vecino o un amigo. Establezca una hora para la tarea y ofrezca a su niño un lugar tranquilo donde trabajar (por ejemplo un lugar sin TV). Anime a su niño a comentar lo que está aprendiendo en la clase de matemáticas. Si su niño tiene problemas con las matemáticas, por favor comuníquese conmigo para indicarle cómo puede ayudarlo.

Muchas gracias. Usted es imprescindible en el aprendizaje de su niño.

Atentamente,
El maestro de su niño

COMMON CORE La Unidad 1 incluye los Common Core Standards for Mathematical Content for Operations and Algebraic Thinking 1.OA.1, 1.OA.3, 1.OA.5, 1.OA.6, 1.OA.8 and all Mathematical Practices.

Por favor complete la siguiente información y devuelva este formulario al maestro.

La persona que ayudará a mi niño _____ es
                                              (nombre del niño)

_____. Esta persona es _____
        (nombre de la persona)   (relación con el niño)

de mi niño.

Discuss Numbers 1–10

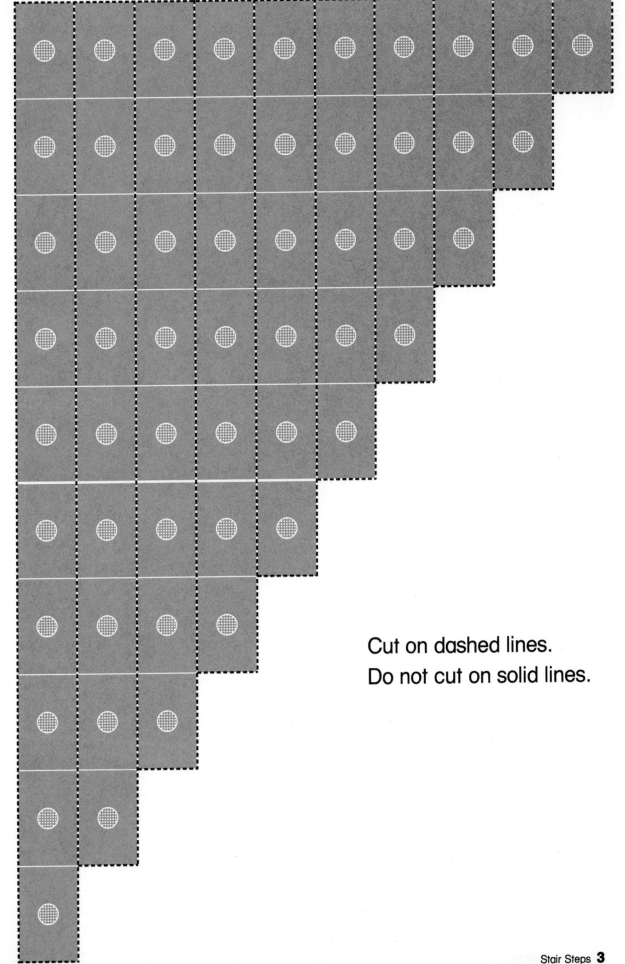

Cut on dashed lines.
Do not cut on solid lines.

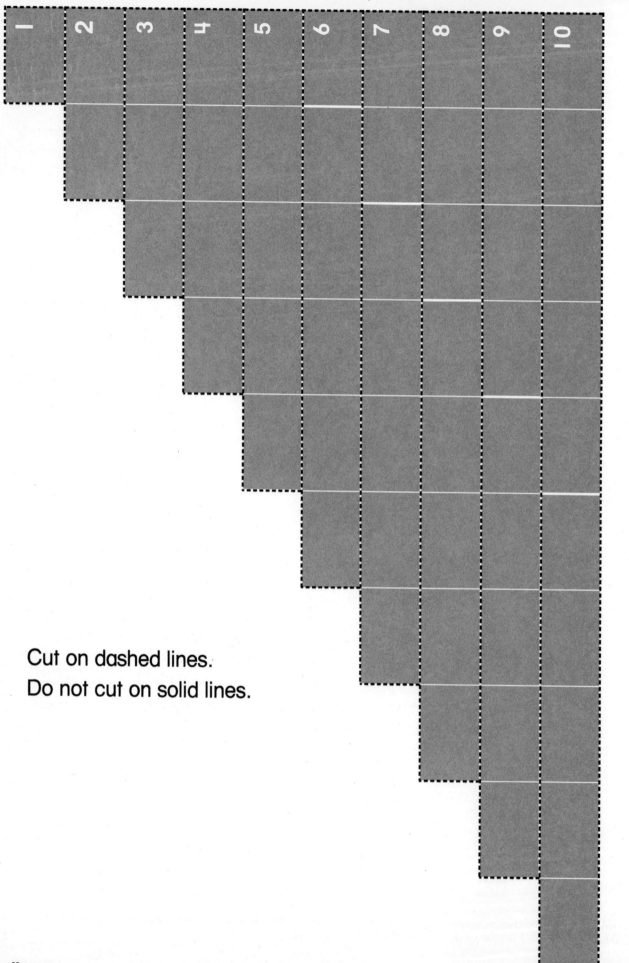

Cut on dashed lines.
Do not cut on solid lines.

Family Letter

Dear Family:

Your child is learning to see numbers as a group of 5 and extra ones. Making mental pictures by grouping units in this way will later help your child add and subtract quickly. Children benefit greatly from learning to "see" numbers without counting every unit.

Children start exploring these 5-groups by looking at dots arranged in a row of 5 plus some extra ones. Below are samples that show the numbers from 6 through 10.

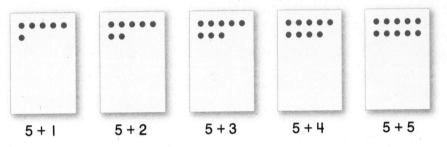

5 + 1   5 + 2   5 + 3   5 + 4   5 + 5

The teacher gives the children a number and asks them to say it as a 5 plus extra ones. Children say the numbers in order at first. Later they can "see" the quantities even when the numbers are shown randomly.

Teacher: What is 6?

Class: 5 + 1

Teacher: What is 7?

Class: 5 + 2

On some homework pages, you will find instructions that ask children to "see the 5." Your child is being encouraged to make a mental picture of a number that contains a 5-group. Later, the children will be asked to see groups of 10 by combining two 5-groups. This will help them learn place value.

It takes repeated exposure to such groups for children to see the numbers quickly. Many of the visual aids in your child's classroom include 5-groups. Children tend to absorb these visual patterns without realizing it.

If you have any questions or problems, please contact me.

Sincerely,
Your child's teacher

COMMON CORE Unit 1 includes the Common Core Standards for Mathematical Content for Operations and Algebraic Thinking 1.OA.1, 1.OA.3, 1.OA.5, 1.OA.6, 1.OA.8 and all Mathematical Practices.

Estimada familia:

Su niño está aprendiendo a ver los números como un grupo de 5 más otras unidades. El hecho de agrupar mentalmente unidades de esa manera ayudará a su niño a sumar y restar rápidamente en el futuro. Los niños se benefician muchísimo de aprender a "ver" los números sin contar cada unidad.

Los niños comienzan a practicar con estos grupos de 5 observando puntos distribuidos en una fila de 5 más otras unidades. Estos ejemplos muestran los números del 6 al 10.

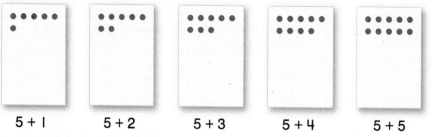

| 5 + 1 | 5 + 2 | 5 + 3 | 5 + 4 | 5 + 5 |

El maestro les da un número a los niños y les pide que lo digan como 5 más otras unidades. Al principio, los niños dicen los números en orden. Más adelante pueden "ver" las cantidades incluso cuando los números se muestran sin un orden específico.

Maestro: ¿Qué es el 6?

Clase: 5 + 1

Maestro: ¿Qué es el 7?

Clase: 5 + 2

En algunas páginas de tarea hallará instrucciones que piden a los niños "ver el número 5". A su niño se le está animando a que visualice un número que contenga un grupo de 5. Más adelante, se les pedirá que vean grupos de 10, combinando dos grupos de 5. Esto les ayudará a aprender el valor posicional.

Es necesario que los niños practiquen muchas veces los grupos de este tipo para que puedan llegar a ver los números rápidamente. Muchas de las ayudas visuales que hay en el salón de clase incluyen grupos de 5. Los niños tienden a absorber estos patrones visuales sin darse cuenta.

Si tiene alguna pregunta o algún comentario, por favor comuníquese conmigo.

Atentamente,
El maestro de su niño

 COMMON CORE

La Unidad 1 incluye los Common Core Standards for Mathematical Content for Operations and Algebraic Thinking 1.OA.1, 1.OA.3, 1.OA.5, 1.OA.6, 1.OA.8 and all Mathematical Practices.

Visualize Numbers as a 5-Group and Ones

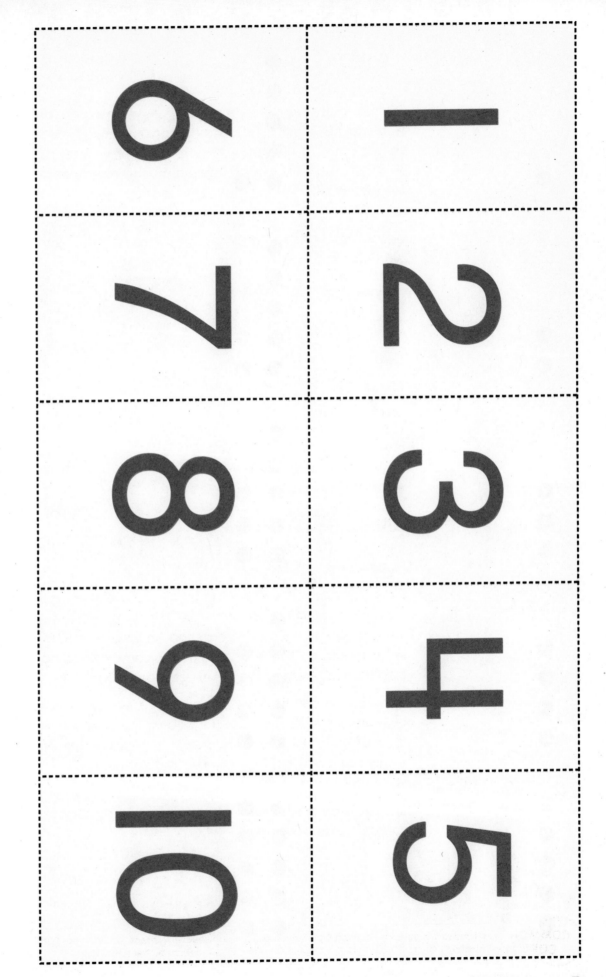

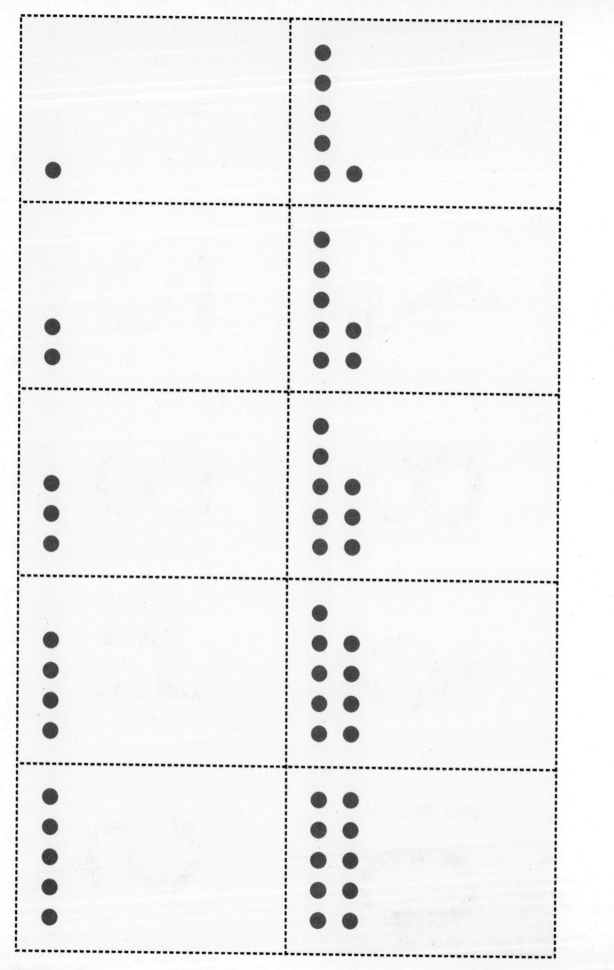

Family Letter

Dear Family:

Your child is learning to find the smaller numbers that are "hiding" inside a larger number. He or she will be participating in activities that will help him or her master addition, subtraction, and equation building.

To make the concepts clear, this program uses some special vocabulary and materials that we would like to share. Below are two important terms that your child is learning:

Partners of 7

- **Partners:** Partners are two numbers that can be put together to make a larger number. For example, 2 and 5 are partners that go together to make the number 7.

- **Break Apart:** Children can "break apart" a larger number to form two smaller numbers. Your child is using objects and drawings to explore ways of "breaking apart" numbers of ten or less.

Children can discover the break-aparts of a number with circle drawings. They first draw the "Break-Apart Stick" and then color the circles to show the different partners, as shown below. Sometimes they also write the partners on a special partner train, which is also shown below.

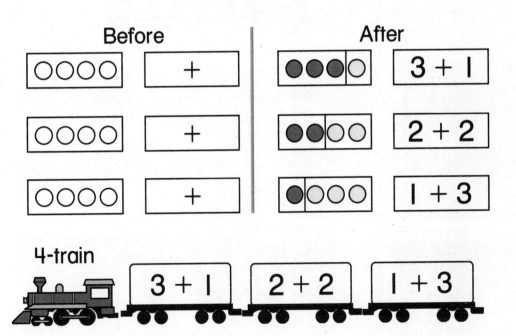

Later, children will discover that partners can change places without changing the total. This concept is called "switch the partners." Once children understand switching partners, they can find the break-aparts of a number more quickly. They simply switch each pair of partners as they discover them.

Shown below are the break-aparts and switched partners of the number 7. Sometimes children also write this information on a double-decker train.

Break-Aparts of 7

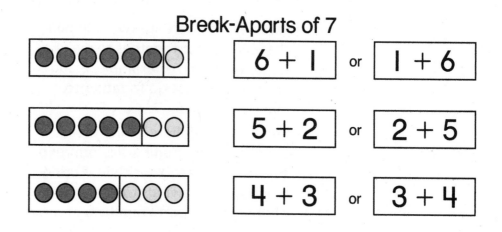

6 + 1 or 1 + 6	
5 + 2 or 2 + 5	
4 + 3 or 3 + 4	

Double-Decker Train

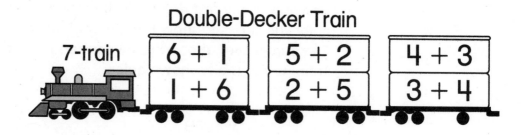

7-train

| 6 + 1 | 5 + 2 | 4 + 3 |
| 1 + 6 | 2 + 5 | 3 + 4 |

You will see the circle drawings and the partner trains on your child's math homework. Be ready to offer help if it is needed. Children are doing these activities in class, but they may still need help at home.

If you have any questions or problems, please talk to me.

Sincerely,
Your child's teacher

COMMON CORE Unit 1 includes the Common Core Standards for Mathematical Content for Operations and Algebraic Thinking 1.OA.1, 1.OA.3, 1.OA.5, 1.OA.6, 1.OA.8 and all Mathematical Practices.

Estimada familia:

Su niño está aprendiendo a hallar los números más pequeños que están "escondidos" dentro de un número más grande. Va a participar en actividades que le ayudarán a dominar la suma, la resta y la formación de ecuaciones.

Para clarificar los conceptos, este programa usa un vocabulario especial y algunos materiales que nos gustaría mostrarle. A continuación hay dos términos importantes que su niño está aprendiendo:

- **Partes:** Partes son dos números que se pueden unir para formar un número más grande. Por ejemplo, 2 y 5 son partes que se unen para formar el número 7.

- **Separar:** Los niños pueden "separar" un número más grande para formar dos números más pequeños. Su niño está usando objetos y dibujos para explorar maneras de "separar" números iguales o menores que diez.

Partes de 7

Los niños pueden separar un número usando dibujos de círculos. Primero dibujan un "palito de separación" y luego colorean los círculos para indicar las partes, como se muestra a continuación. A veces los niños anotan las partes en un tren de partes especial, que también se muestra a continuación.

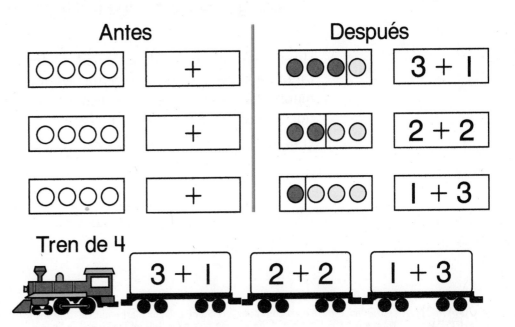

Luego, los niños van a aprender que las partes pueden intercambiar su posición sin que varíe el total. Este concepto se llama "cambiar el orden de las partes". Una vez que los niños entienden el cambio del orden de las partes, pueden encontrar las partes de un número con más rapidez. Sencillamente cambian cada par de partes a medida que las encuentran.

A continuación están las partes, y las partes en otro orden, del número 7. A veces los niños escriben esta información en un tren de dos pisos.

Partes de 7

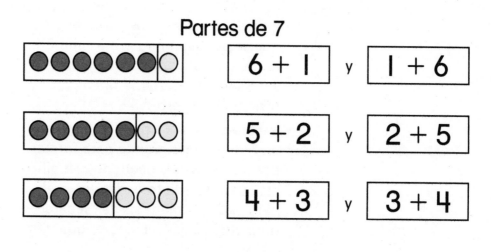

| $6 + 1$ | y | $1 + 6$ |

| $5 + 2$ | y | $2 + 5$ |

| $4 + 3$ | y | $3 + 4$ |

Tren de dos pisos

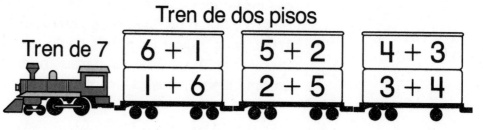

Tren de 7

| $6 + 1$ | $5 + 2$ | $4 + 3$ |
| $1 + 6$ | $2 + 5$ | $3 + 4$ |

Usted verá los dibujos de los círculos y los trenes de partes en la tarea de matemáticas de su niño. Ayúdelo, si es necesario. Los niños están haciendo estas actividades en clase, pero es posible que aún así necesiten ayuda en casa.

Si tiene preguntas o dudas, por favor comuníquese conmigo.

Atentamente,
El maestro de su niño

La Unidad 1 incluye los Common Core Standards for Mathematical Content for Operations and Algebraic Thinking 1.OA.1, 1.OA.3, 1.OA.5, 1.OA.6, 1.OA.8 and all Mathematical Practices.

Partners of 2 Through 5

Name _____

Write the **partners**.

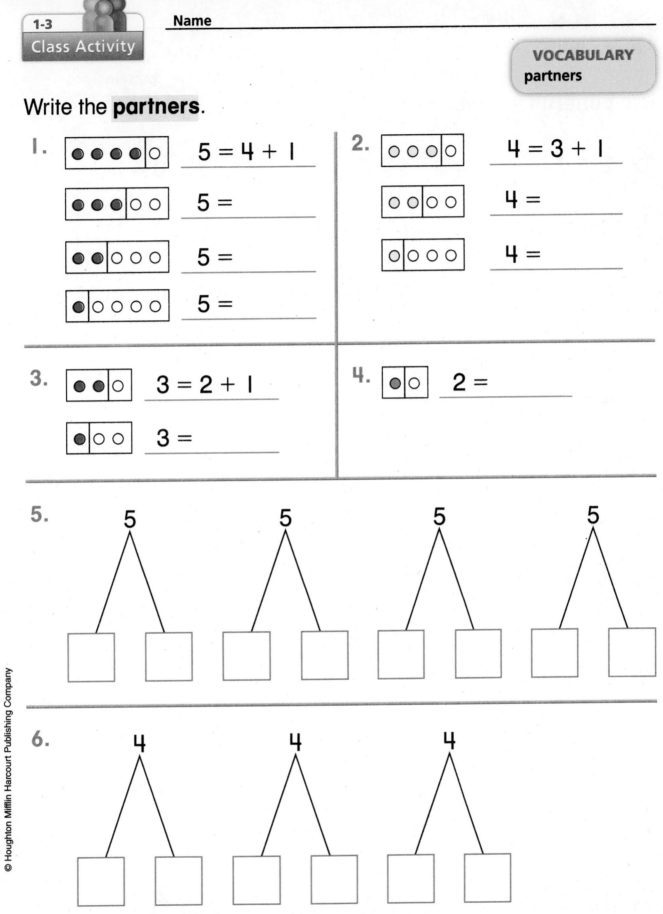

1. $5 = 4 + 1$

   $5 =$ _____

   $5 =$ _____

   $5 =$ _____

2. $4 = 3 + 1$

   $4 =$ _____

   $4 =$ _____

3. $3 = 2 + 1$

   $3 =$ _____

4. $2 =$ _____

5. 5   5   5   5

6. 4   4   4

VOCABULARY
patterns

Use **patterns** to solve.

7. 2 + 0 = ☐   5 + 0 = ☐   3 + 0 = ☐

    4 + 0 = ☐   1 + 0 = ☐   0 + 3 = ☐

    0 + 5 = ☐   0 + 2 = ☐   0 + 4 = ☐

8. 4 + 1 = ☐   2 + 1 = ☐   3 + 1 = ☐

    1 + 1 = ☐   1 + 4 = ☐   1 + 3 = ☐

9. 2 + 2 = ☐   3 + 2 = ☐   1 + 2 = ☐

10. 2 − 0 = ☐   5 − 0 = ☐   3 − 0 = ☐

11. 5 − 1 = ☐   3 − 1 = ☐   4 − 1 = ☐

12. 4 − 2 = ☐   3 − 2 = ☐   5 − 2 = ☐

1. Show and write the 6-partners.

⊕⊕⊕⊕⊕⊕	+	6 = _____
⊕⊕⊕⊕⊕⊕	+	6 = _____
⊕⊕⊕⊕⊕⊕	+	6 = _____
⊕⊕⊕⊕⊕⊕	+	6 = _____
⊕⊕⊕⊕⊕	+	6 = _____

2. Write the 6-partners.

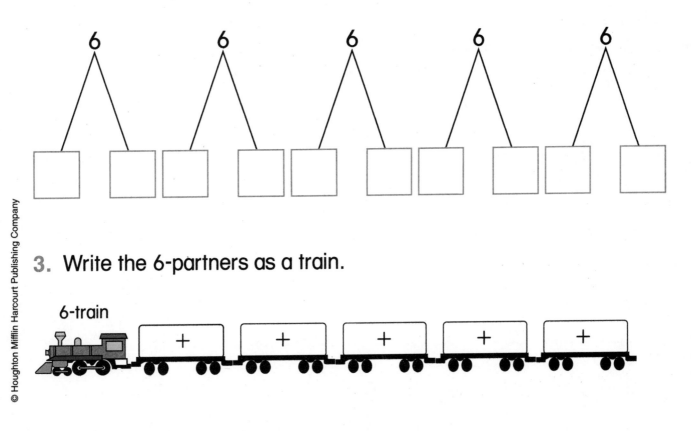

3. Write the 6-partners as a train.

6-train

VOCABULARY
doubles

4. Discuss patterns in the partners.

2	**3**	**4**	**5**	**6**
1 + 1	2 + 1	3 + 1	4 + 1	5 + 1
		2 + 2	3 + 2	4 + 2
				3 + 3

Use **doubles** to solve.

5. 3 + 3 = ☐   1 + 1 = ☐   2 + 2 = ☐

   6 − 3 = ☐   2 − 1 = ☐   4 − 2 = ☐

Use patterns to solve.

6. 6 + 0 = ☐   0 + 4 = ☐   1 + 0 = ☐

   0 + 3 = ☐   2 + 0 = ☐   0 + 5 = ☐

7. 4 − 0 = ☐   2 − 0 = ☐   6 − 0 = ☐

   5 − 0 = ☐   1 − 0 = ☐   3 − 0 = ☐

8. 3 − 3 = ☐   5 − 5 = ☐   1 − 1 = ☐

   4 − 4 = ☐   2 − 2 = ☐   6 − 6 = ☐

Partners of 6

Name _____

Show the 7-partners and **switch the partners**.

1. ○○○○○○○   [+] and [+]

2. ○○○○○○○   [+] and [+]

3. ○○○○○○○   [+] and [+]

Write the partners and the switched partners.

4.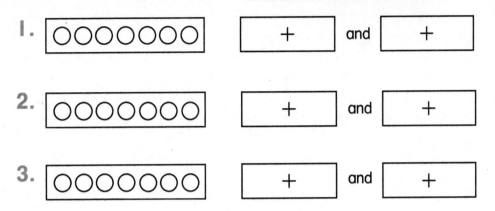
7-train

5.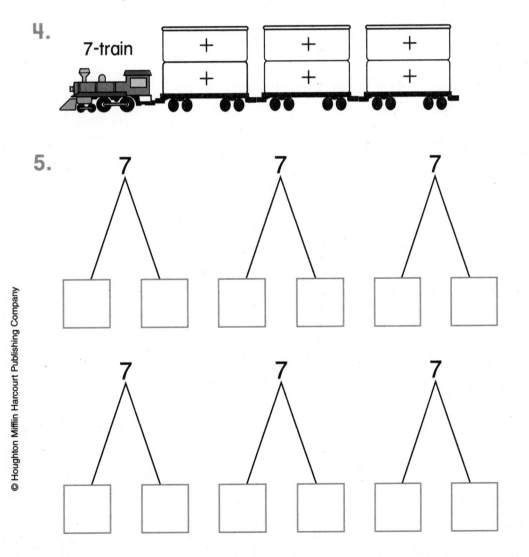

© Houghton Mifflin Harcourt Publishing Company

6. Discuss patterns in the partners.

2	3	4	5	6	7
1 + 1	2 + 1	3 + 1	4 + 1	5 + 1	6 + 1
		2 + 2	3 + 2	4 + 2	5 + 2
				3 + 3	4 + 3

Use patterns to solve.

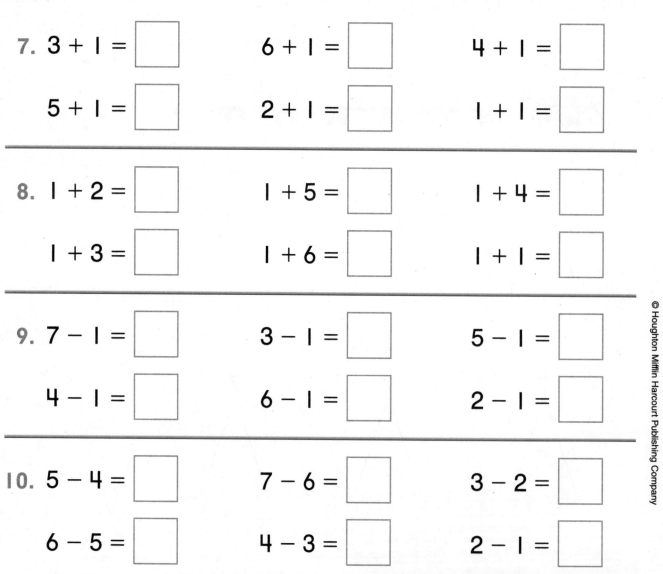

7. 3 + 1 = ☐   6 + 1 = ☐   4 + 1 = ☐

5 + 1 = ☐   2 + 1 = ☐   1 + 1 = ☐

8. 1 + 2 = ☐   1 + 5 = ☐   1 + 4 = ☐

1 + 3 = ☐   1 + 6 = ☐   1 + 1 = ☐

9. 7 − 1 = ☐   3 − 1 = ☐   5 − 1 = ☐

4 − 1 = ☐   6 − 1 = ☐   2 − 1 = ☐

10. 5 − 4 = ☐   7 − 6 = ☐   3 − 2 = ☐

6 − 5 = ☐   4 − 3 = ☐   2 − 1 = ☐

Show the 8-partners and switch the partners.

1. ☐ ⭕⭕⭕⭕⭕⭕⭕⭕ ☐ [+] and [+]

2. ☐ ⭕⭕⭕⭕⭕⭕⭕⭕ ☐ [+] and [+]

3. ☐ ⭕⭕⭕⭕⭕⭕⭕⭕ ☐ [+] and [+]

4. ☐ ⭕⭕⭕⭕⭕⭕⭕⭕ ☐ [+] and [+]

Write the partners and the switched partners.

5.

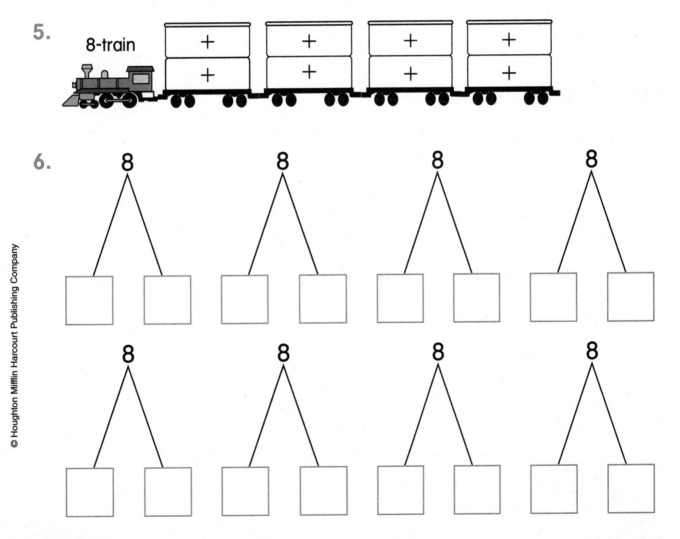

8-train

| + | + | + | + |
| + | + | + | + |

6.

8 / \ ☐ ☐   8 / \ ☐ ☐   8 / \ ☐ ☐   8 / \ ☐ ☐

8 / \ ☐ ☐   8 / \ ☐ ☐   8 / \ ☐ ☐   8 / \ ☐ ☐

Name

7. Discuss patterns in the partners.

2	3	4	5	6	7	8
1 + 1	2 + 1	3 + 1	4 + 1	5 + 1	6 + 1	7 + 1
	2 + 2	3 + 2	4 + 2	5 + 2	6 + 2
			3 + 3	4 + 3	5 + 3
					4 + 4

Use doubles to solve.

8. 4 + 4 = ☐   3 + 3 = ☐   2 + 2 = ☐

8 − 4 = ☐   6 − 3 = ☐   4 − 2 = ☐

Use patterns to solve.

9. 8 + 0 = ☐   6 + 0 = ☐   7 + 0 = ☐

0 + 5 = ☐   0 + 3 = ☐   0 + 4 = ☐

10. 7 − 0 = ☐   2 − 0 = ☐   8 − 0 = ☐

5 − 0 = ☐   3 − 0 = ☐   6 − 0 = ☐

11. 4 − 4 = ☐   6 − 6 = ☐   2 − 2 = ☐

8 − 8 = ☐   7 − 7 = ☐   5 − 5 = ☐

Partners of 8

Show the 9-partners and switch the partners.

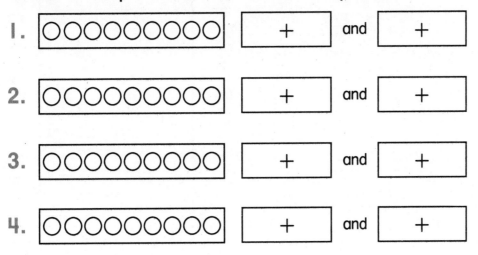

1. ⎕OOOOOOOOO [+] and [+]

2. ⎕OOOOOOOOO [+] and [+]

3. ⎕OOOOOOOOO [+] and [+]

4. ⎕OOOOOOOOO [+] and [+]

Write the partners and the switched partners.

5.

9-train

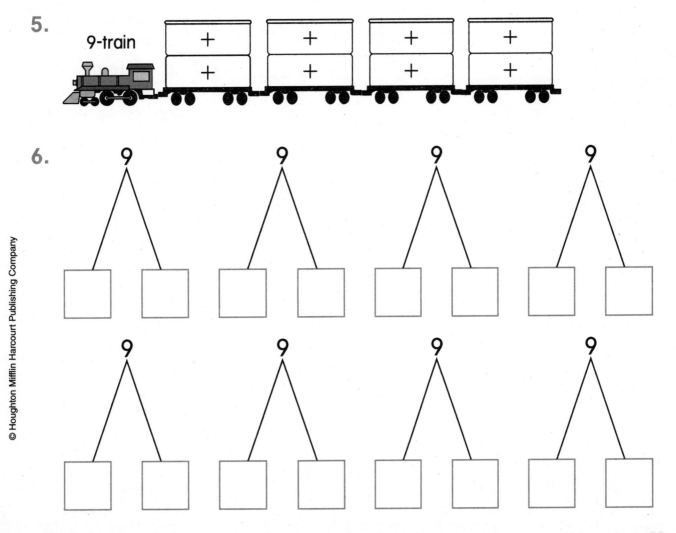

6.

7. Discuss patterns in the partners.

2	**3**	**4**	**5**	**6**	**7**	**8**	**9**
1 + 1	2 + 1	3 + 1	4 + 1	5 + 1	6 + 1	7 + 1	8 + 1
	2 + 2	3 + 2	4 + 2	5 + 2	6 + 2	7 + 2
		3 + 3	4 + 3	5 + 3	6 + 3
			4 + 4	5 + 4

Use patterns to solve.

8. 6 + 1 = ☐   8 + 1 = ☐

4 + 1 = ☐   3 + 1 = ☐

5 + 1 = ☐   7 + 1 = ☐

9. 1 + 7 = ☐   1 + 2 = ☐

1 + 8 = ☐   1 + 4 = ☐

1 + 6 = ☐   1 + 5 = ☐

10. 9 – 1 = ☐   3 – 1 = ☐

7 – 1 = ☐   6 – 1 = ☐

8 – 1 = ☐   5 – 1 = ☐

11. 9 – 8 = ☐   3 – 2 = ☐

7 – 6 = ☐   6 – 5 = ☐

8 – 7 = ☐   5 – 4 = ☐

1. Discuss patterns.

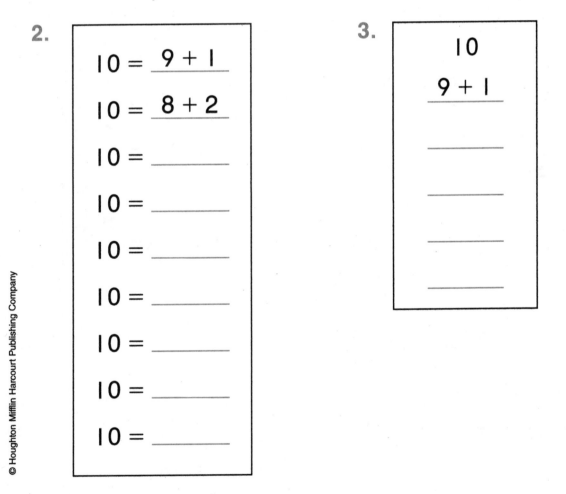

Partners of 10

9 + 1   8 + 2   7 + 3   6 + 4   5 + 5

1 + 9   2 + 8   3 + 7   4 + 6

Write the 10-partners.

2.

10 = _9 + 1_

10 = _8 + 2_

10 = _____

10 = _____

10 = _____

10 = _____

10 = _____

10 = _____

10 = _____

3.

10

9 + 1

_____

_____

_____

_____

_____

Name _____

4. Discuss patterns.

Patterns with Partners

2	3	4	5	6	7	8	9	10
1+1	2+1	3+1	4+1	5+1	6+1	7+1	8+1	9+1
		2+2	3+2	4+2	5+2	6+2	7+2	8+2
				3+3	4+3	5+3	6+3	7+3
						4+4	5+4	6+4
								5+5

Patterns with Zero

1+0=1	1-0=1	1-1=0
2+0=2	2-0=2	2-2=0
3+0=3	3-0=3	3-3=0
4+0=4	4-0=4	4-4=0
5+0=5	5-0=5	5-5=0
6+0=6	6-0=6	6-6=0
7+0=7	7-0=7	7-7=0
8+0=8	8-0=8	8-8=0
9+0=9	9-0=9	9-9=0
10+0=10	10-0=10	10-10=0

Patterns with Doubles

1+1=2
2+2=4
3+3=6
4+4=8
5+5=10

Name _____

▶ **Math and a Marching Band**

Write the number of band members in each row.

1.

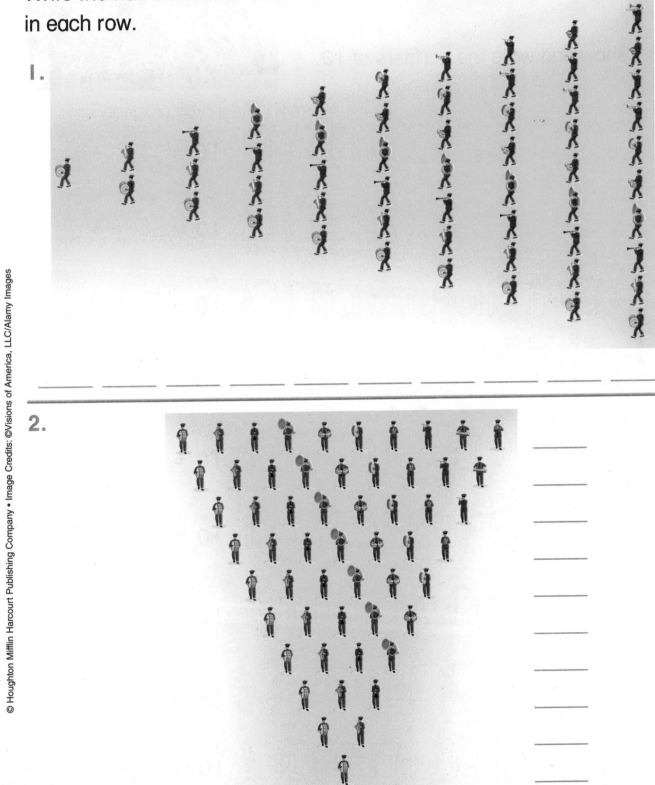

_____ _____ _____ _____ _____ _____ _____ _____ _____

2.

_____

_____

_____

_____

_____

_____

_____

_____

_____

Name

3. Show and write the partners of 10.

10 = _____ + _____

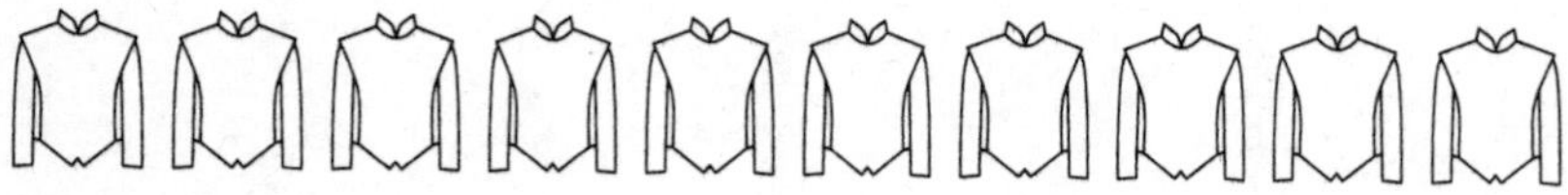

10 = _____ + _____

10 = _____ + _____

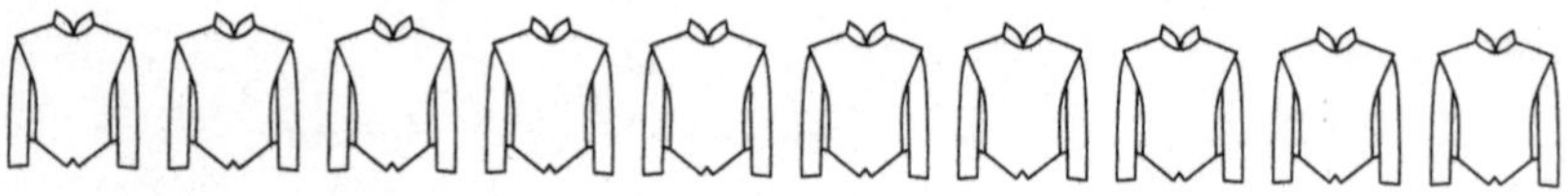

10 = _____ + _____

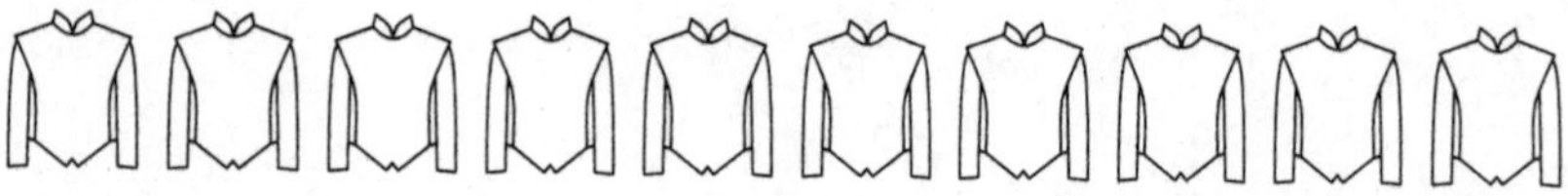

10 = _____ + _____

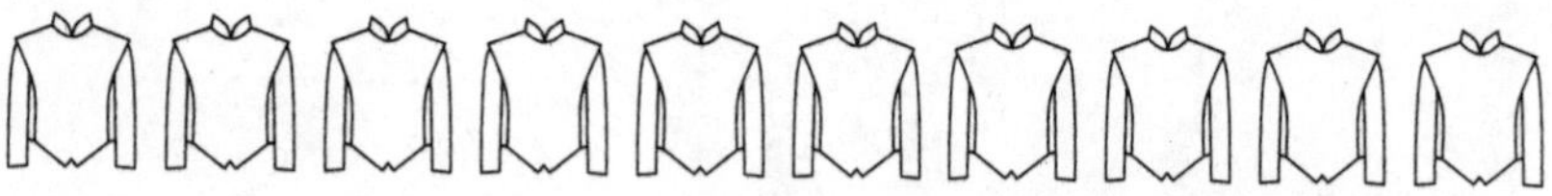

10 = _____ + _____

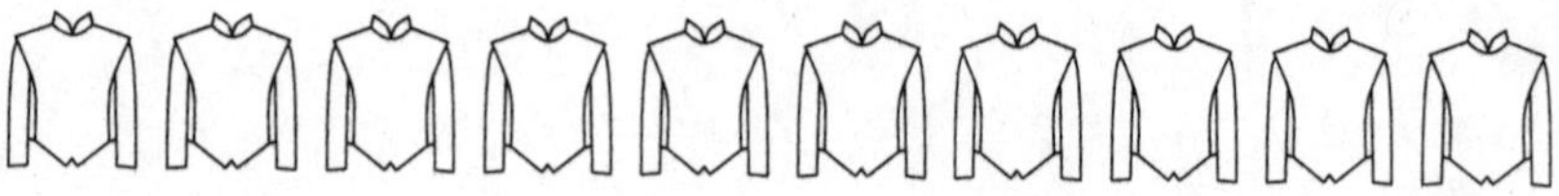

10 = _____ + _____

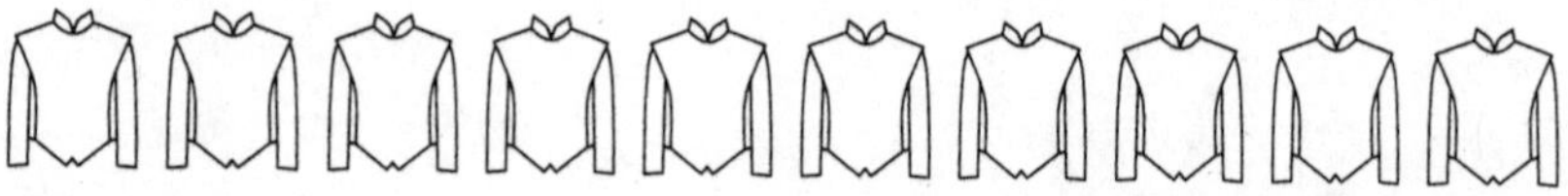

10 = _____ + _____

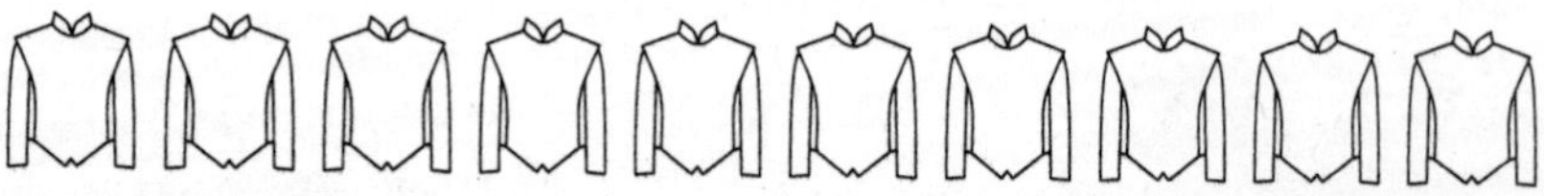

10 = _____ + _____

Focus on Mathematical Practices

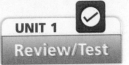
See the 5-group.
Draw extra dots to show the number.

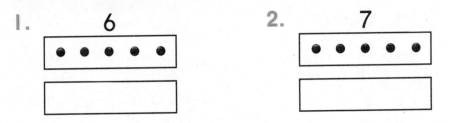

1. 6

2. 7

Write how many dots. See the 5 in each group.

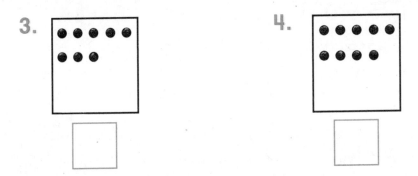

3.

4.

Write the 10-partners and switch the partners.

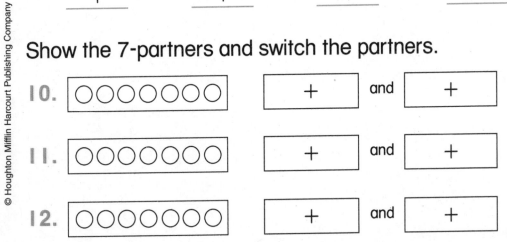

5. ___ + ___

___ + ___

6. ___ + ___

___ + ___

7. ___ + ___

___ + ___

8. ___ + ___

___ + ___

9. ___ + ___

___ + ___

Show the 7-partners and switch the partners.

10. ○○○○○○○   ___ + ___   and   ___ + ___

11. ○○○○○○○   ___ + ___   and   ___ + ___

12. ○○○○○○○   ___ + ___   and   ___ + ___

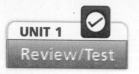
Use patterns to solve.

13. 5 + 0 = ☐   14. 0 + 6 = ☐   15. 8 + 0 = ☐

16. 7 + 1 = ☐   17. 1 + 5 = ☐   18. 9 + 1 = ☐

19. 6 − 0 = ☐   20. 5 − 0 = ☐   21. 7 − 0 = ☐

22. 4 − 1 = ☐   23. 9 − 1 = ☐   24. 8 − 1 = ☐

25. **Extended Response** Draw a story about a set of 8-partners. Write the partners.

Dear Family:

Your child has started a new unit on addition, subtraction, and equations. These concepts are introduced with stories that capture children's interest and help them to see adding and subtracting as real-life processes.

At the beginning of the unit, children show a story problem by drawing a picture of the objects. If they are adding 4 balloons and 2 balloons, for example, their pictures might look like the top one shown here. If they are subtracting, their pictures might look like the bottom one.

Addition

Subtraction

In a short time, children will show objects quickly with circles rather than pictures. This is a major conceptual advance because it requires the use of symbols. Children are asked to show the partners (4 + 2) as well as give the total (6). From here, children are just a small step away from writing standard equations, such as $4 + 2 = 6$ and $6 - 4 = 2$.

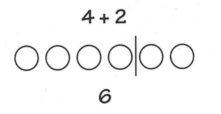

4 + 2

6

Addition Problem

6 – 4

2

Subtraction Problem

To keep them focused on the actual problem, children are often asked to give a "complete answer" in class. This means that they should name the objects as well as give the number. Right now, complete answers are not required for homework. Even so, it would be helpful for you to ask your child to say the complete answer when working with you at home. Example: "You said the answer is 6. Is it 6 dinosaurs? No? Then 6 what? . . . Oh! 6 balloons!"

Sincerely,
Your child's teacher

© Houghton Mifflin Harcourt Publishing Company

COMMON CORE

Unit 2 includes the Common Core Standards for Mathematical Content for Operations and Algebraic Thinking, 1.OA.1, 1.OA.3, 1.OA.5, 1.OA.6, 1.OA.7, 1.OA.8 and all Mathematical Practices.

Estimada familia:

Su niño ha empezado una nueva unidad sobre la suma, la resta y las ecuaciones. Estos conceptos se presentan con cuentos que captan el interés de los niños y les ayudan a ver la suma y la resta como procesos de la vida diaria.

Al comienzo de la unidad, los niños muestran un problema en forma de cuento haciendo un dibujo de los objetos. Por ejemplo, si están sumando 4 globos y 2 globos, sus dibujos pueden parecerse al dibujo de arriba. Si están restando, es posible que sus dibujos se parezcan al dibujo de abajo.

Suma

Al poco tiempo, los niños mostrarán objetos rápidamente con círculos en vez de dibujos. Esto es un gran paso conceptual, ya que requiere el uso de signos.

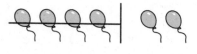

Resta

A los niños se les pide que muestren las partes (4 + 2) y la respuesta (6). Una vez que hacen esto, están casi listos para escribir ecuaciones normales, tales como 4 + 2 = 6 y 6 − 4 = 2.

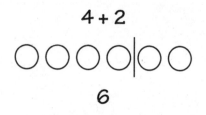

$$4 + 2$$

6

Problema de suma

$$6 - 4$$

2

Problema de resta

Para que sigan concentrándose en el problema mismo, a los niños se les pide una "respuesta completa" en la clase. Esto significa que deben nombrar los objetos y dar el número. Actualmente, no se requieren respuestas completas en la tarea. Sin embargo, sería de ayuda si le pidiera a su niño que le dé la respuesta completa cuando trabaja con Ud. en casa. Por ejemplo: "Dijiste que la respuesta es 6. ¿Son 6 dinosaurios? ¿No? Entonces, ¿6 de qué?... ¡Ajá! ¡6 globos!"

Atentamente,
El maestro de su niño

COMMON CORE La Unidad 2 incluye los Common Core Standards for Mathematical Content for Operations and Algebraic Thinking, 1.OA.1, 1.OA.3, 1.OA.5, 1.OA.6, 1.OA.7, 1.OA.8 and all Mathematical Practices.

Represent Addition

Write the **partners** and the **total**.

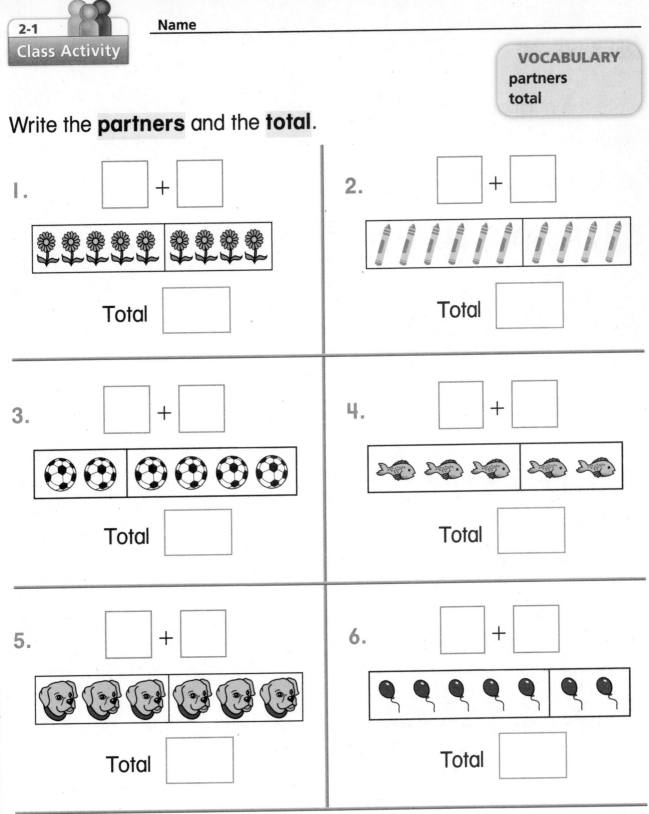

1. ☐ + ☐

    Total ☐

2. ☐ + ☐

    Total ☐

3. ☐ + ☐

    Total ☐

4. ☐ + ☐

    Total ☐

5. ☐ + ☐

    Total ☐

6. ☐ + ☐

    Total ☐

7. Draw a picture of flowers to show 4 + 2. Write the total.

Write the partners and the total.

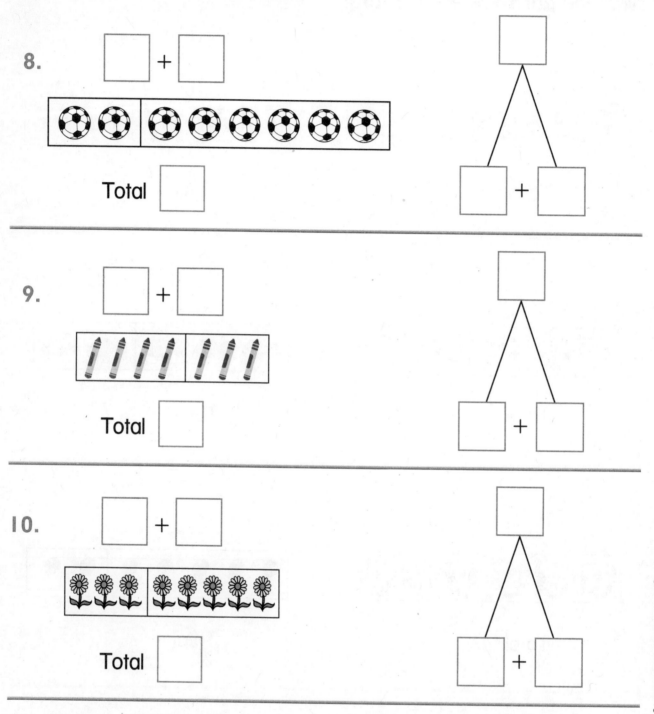

8. ☐ + ☐

Total ☐

9. ☐ + ☐

Total ☐

10. ☐ + ☐

Total ☐

11. Draw a Math Mountain to show 6 + 2.
Write the total.

Represent Addition

Name _____

Write the partners and total for each **circle drawing**.

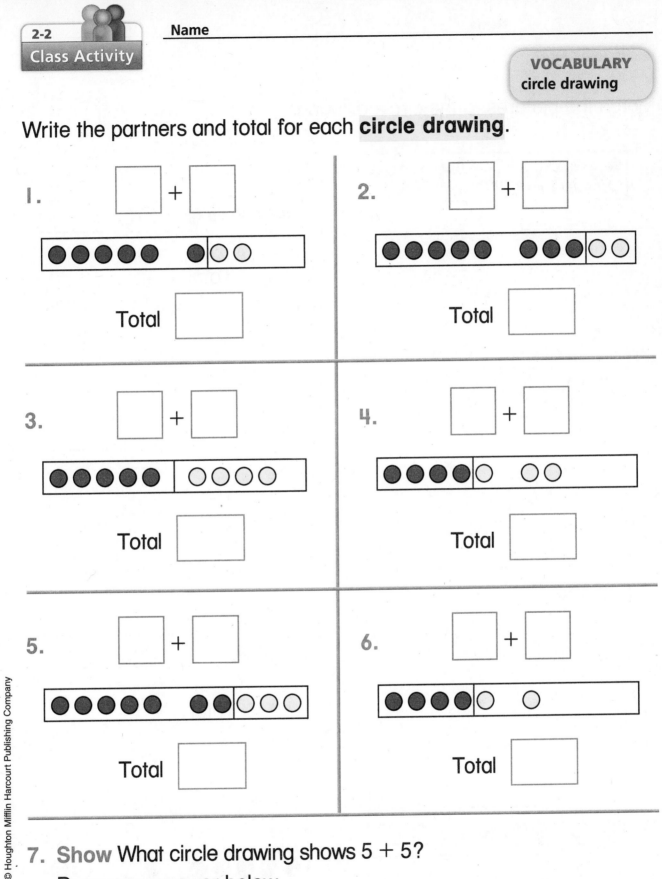

1. ☐ + ☐

Total ☐

2. ☐ + ☐

Total ☐

3. ☐ + ☐

Total ☐

4. ☐ + ☐

Total ☐

5. ☐ + ☐

Total ☐

6. ☐ + ☐

Total ☐

7. **Show** What circle drawing shows $5 + 5$?

Draw your answer below.

Match the pictures to the circle drawings.

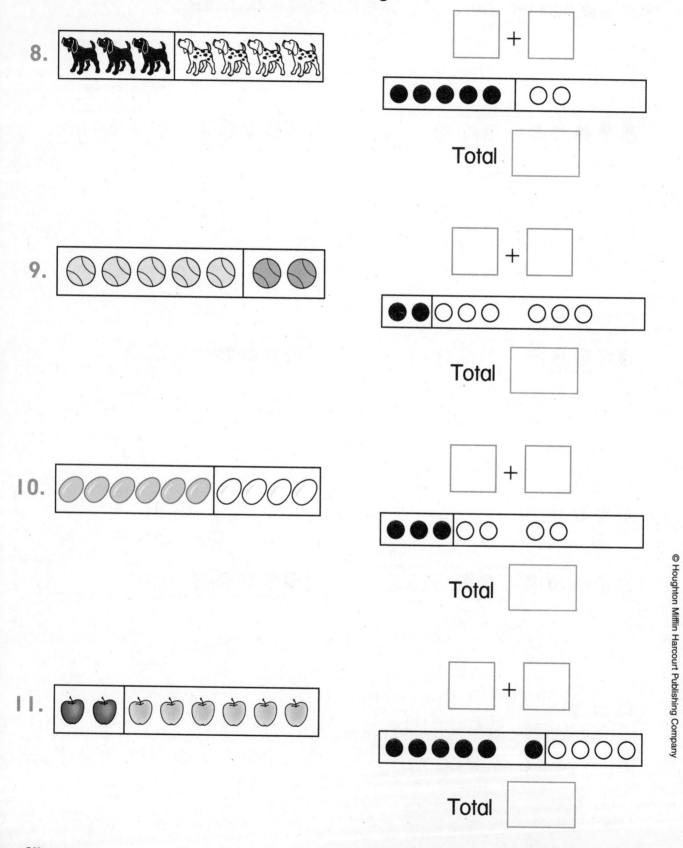

8.

☐ + ☐

Total ☐

9.

☐ + ☐

Total ☐

10.

☐ + ☐

Total ☐

11.

☐ + ☐

Total ☐

Write the partners and the total. Then write the **equation**.

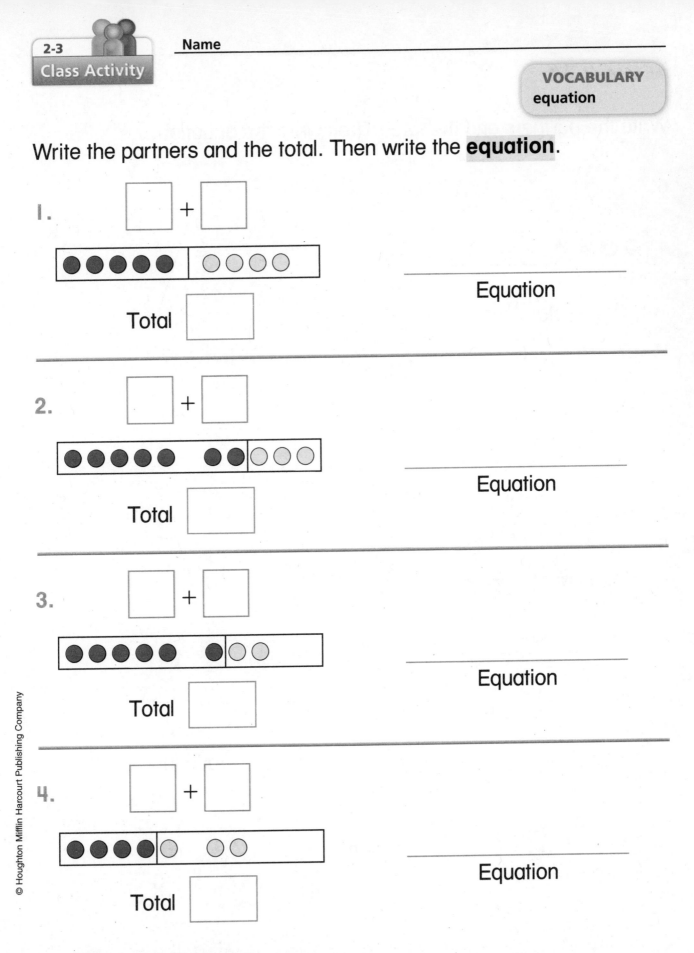

1. ☐ + ☐

Total ☐

_____
Equation

2. ☐ + ☐

Total ☐

_____
Equation

3. ☐ + ☐

Total ☐

_____
Equation

4. ☐ + ☐

Total ☐

_____
Equation

5. Write an equation of your own. _____

Write the partners and the total. Then write the equation.

6.

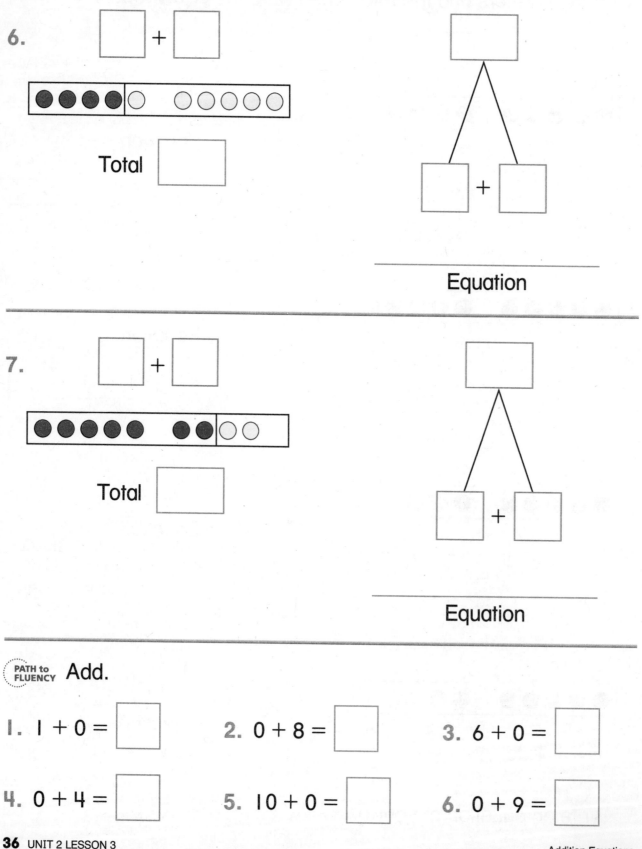

Total

Equation

7.

Total

Equation

PATH to FLUENCY **Add.**

1. $1 + 0 =$ ☐

2. $0 + 8 =$ ☐

3. $6 + 0 =$ ☐

4. $0 + 4 =$ ☐

5. $10 + 0 =$ ☐

6. $0 + 9 =$ ☐

Addition Equations

Dear Family:

Earlier in the unit, your child solved addition problems by making math drawings and counting every object. This is called *counting all*. Now your child is learning a faster strategy that allows them to work directly with numbers. The method they are learning is called *counting on*. It is explained below.

In an addition problem such as 5 + 4, children say (or "think") the first number as if they had already counted it. Then they count on from there. The last number they say is the total. Children can keep track by raising a finger or making a dot for each number as they count on. The diagram below shows both the finger method and the dot method.

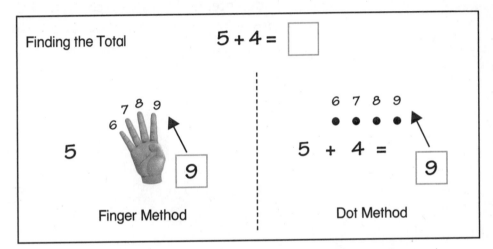

Counting on requires repeated practice. This is provided in class activities and homework assignments. Right now, your child is learning how to find unknown totals. In the next unit, he or she will learn to use the Counting On strategy to subtract.

Counting on is a temporary method to help children build fluency with addition and subtraction within 10. The goal by the end of the grade is for children to automatically know the answer when the total is 10 or less.

Sincerely,
Your child's teacher

© Houghton Mifflin Harcourt Publishing Company

COMMON CORE Unit 2 includes the Common Core Standards for Mathematical Content for Operations and Algebraic Thinking, 1.OA.1, 1.OA.3, 1.OA.5, 1.OA.6, 1.OA.7, 1.OA.8 and all Mathematical Practices.

Estimada familia:

Un poco antes en la unidad su niño resolvió problemas de suma haciendo dibujos matemáticos y contando todos los objetos. A esto se le llama *contar todo*. Ahora su niño está aprendiendo una estrategia más rápida que le permite trabajar directamente con los números. El método que está aprendiendo se llama *contar hacia adelante*. Se explica a continuación.

En un problema de suma, como 5 + 4, los niños dicen (o "piensan") el primer número como si ya lo hubieran contado. Luego cuentan hacia adelante a partir de él. El último número que dicen es el total. Los niños pueden llevar la cuenta levantando un dedo o haciendo un punto por cada número mientras cuentan hacia adelante. El diagrama a continuación muestra tanto el método de los dedos como el de los puntos.

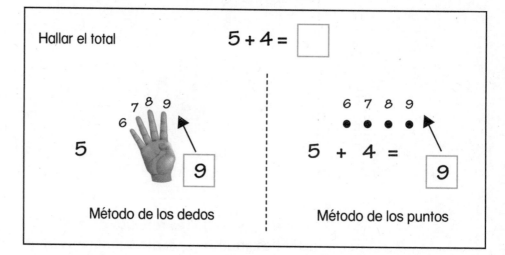

Contar hacia adelante requiere práctica. Esto sucede en las actividades de clase y tareas. En esta unidad, su niño está aprendiendo a hallar un total desconocido. En la próxima unidad, aprenderá a usar la estrategia de contar hacia adelante para restar.

Contar hacia adelante es un método que sirve como ayuda para que los niños dominen la suma y la resta en operaciones hasta el 10. La meta es lograr que al final del año escolar sepan automáticamente la respuesta cuando el total sea 10 ó menos

Atentamente,
El maestro de su niño

 La Unidad 2 incluye los Common Core Standards for Mathematical Content for Operations and Algebraic Thinking, 1.OA.1, 1.OA.3, 1.OA.5, 1.OA.6, 1.OA.7, 1.OA.8 and all Mathematical Practices.

38 UNIT 2 LESSON 5

Explore Solution Methods

Count on to find the total.

1. 4 + 3 = ☐   2. 6 + 4 = ☐   3. 6 + 2 = ☐

4. 4 + 5 = ☐   5. 5 + 3 = ☐   6. 8 + 2 = ☐

7. 2 + 3 = ☐   8. 7 + 3 = ☐   9. 4 + 2 = ☐

Find the total number of toys.

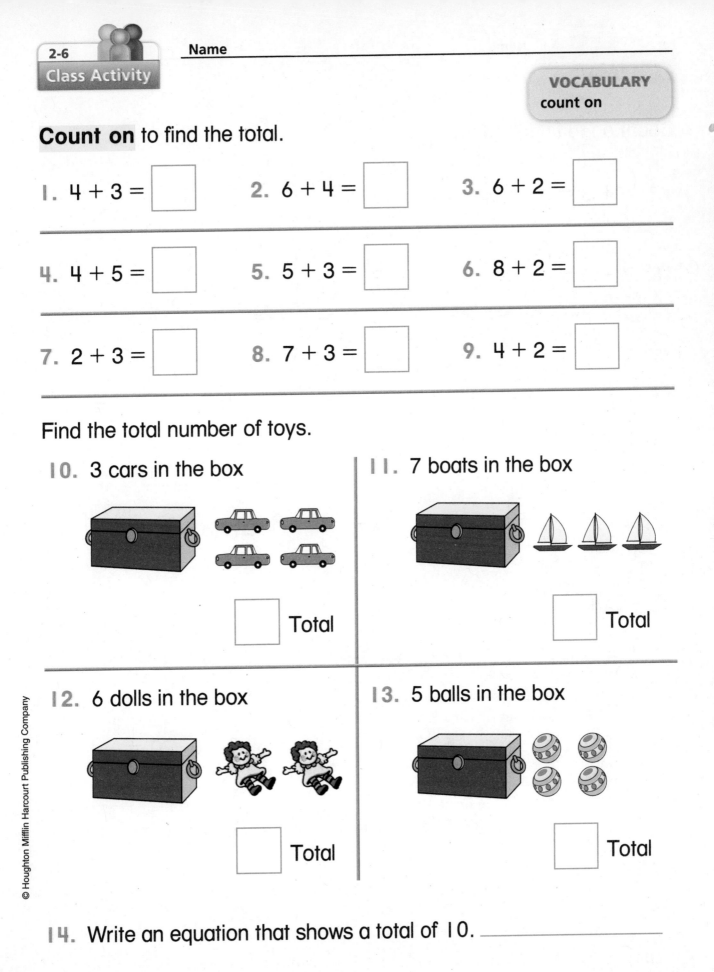

10. 3 cars in the box

☐ Total

11. 7 boats in the box

☐ Total

12. 6 dolls in the box

☐ Total

13. 5 balls in the box

☐ Total

14. Write an equation that shows a total of 10. _____

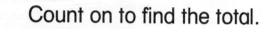
Count on to find the total.

15. $6 + 3 =$ ☐   16. $5 + 2 =$ ☐   17. $7 + 2 =$ ☐

18. $7 + 3 =$ ☐   19. $4 + 3 =$ ☐   20. $4 + 5 =$ ☐

21. $8 + 2 =$ ☐   22. $5 + 2 =$ ☐   23. $4 + 2 =$ ☐

24. $5 + 3 =$ ☐   25. $7 + 2 =$ ☐   26. $7 + 3 =$ ☐

27. $6 + 2 =$ ☐   28. $6 + 4 =$ ☐   29. $3 + 4 =$ ☐

PATH to FLUENCY Add.

1. $7 + 0 =$ ☐   2. $1 + 8 =$ ☐   3. $0 + 8 =$ ☐

4. $9 + 0 =$ ☐   5. $7 + 1 =$ ☐   6. $10 + 0 =$ ☐

7. $6 + 1 =$ ☐   8. $8 + 0 =$ ☐   9. $8 + 1 =$ ☐

10. $9 + 1 =$ ☐   11. $0 + 7 =$ ☐   12. $1 + 7 =$ ☐

Name _____

Underline the greater number.
Count on from that number.

1. 3 + _7_ = ☐

2. 4 + 5 = ☐

3. 2 + 6 = ☐

4. 5 + 3 = ☐

5. 7 + 2 = ☐

6. 3 + 6 = ☐

7. 5 + 2 = ☐

8. 2 + 8 = ☐

9. 7 + 3 = ☐

10. 6 + 3 = ☐

11. **Tell Why** Show two ways to count on to find the total of 6 + 3. Which is faster?

Underline the greater number.
Count on from that number.

12. $\underline{5} + 2 =$ □

13. $7 + 3 =$ □

14. $6 + 2 =$ □

15. $5 + 3 =$ □

16. $3 + 4 =$ □

17. $2 + 7 =$ □

18. $6 + 3 =$ □

19. $8 + 2 =$ □

20. $4 + 3 =$ □

21. $2 + 5 =$ □

22. $5 + 4 =$ □

23. $3 + 5 =$ □

24. $4 + 6 =$ □

25. $2 + 8 =$ □

26. **Explain** How did you solve Exercise 17?

Count On from the Greater Number

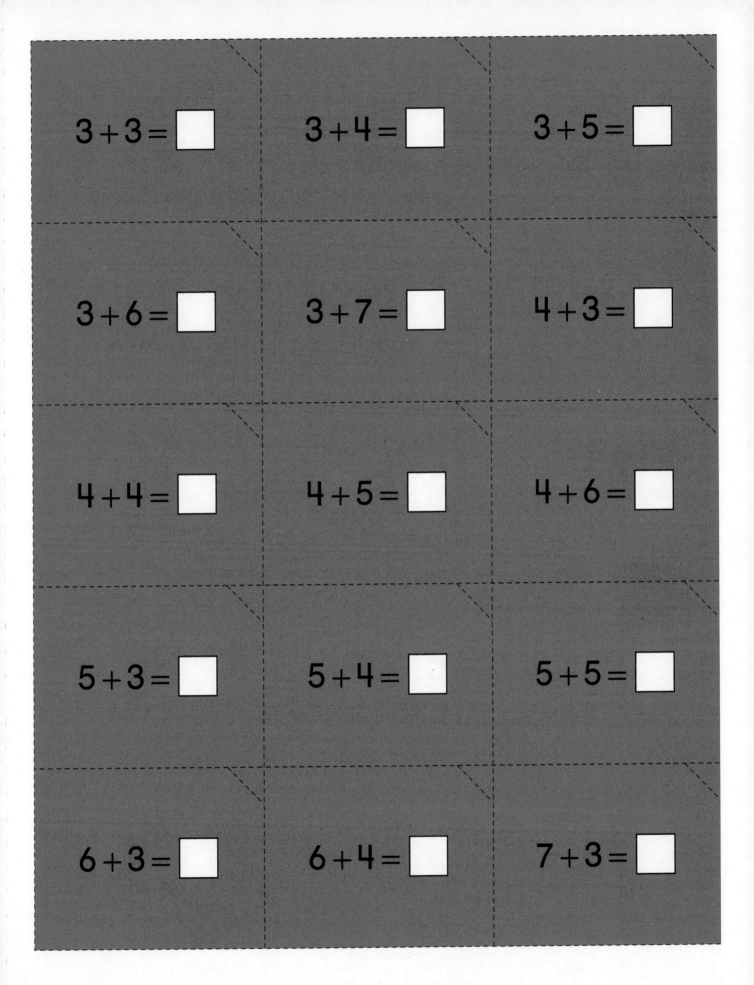

$3+3=$ ☐ $3+4=$ ☐ $3+5=$ ☐

$3+6=$ ☐ $3+7=$ ☐ $4+3=$ ☐

$4+4=$ ☐ $4+5=$ ☐ $4+6=$ ☐

$5+3=$ ☐ $5+4=$ ☐ $5+5=$ ☐

$6+3=$ ☐ $6+4=$ ☐ $7+3=$ ☐

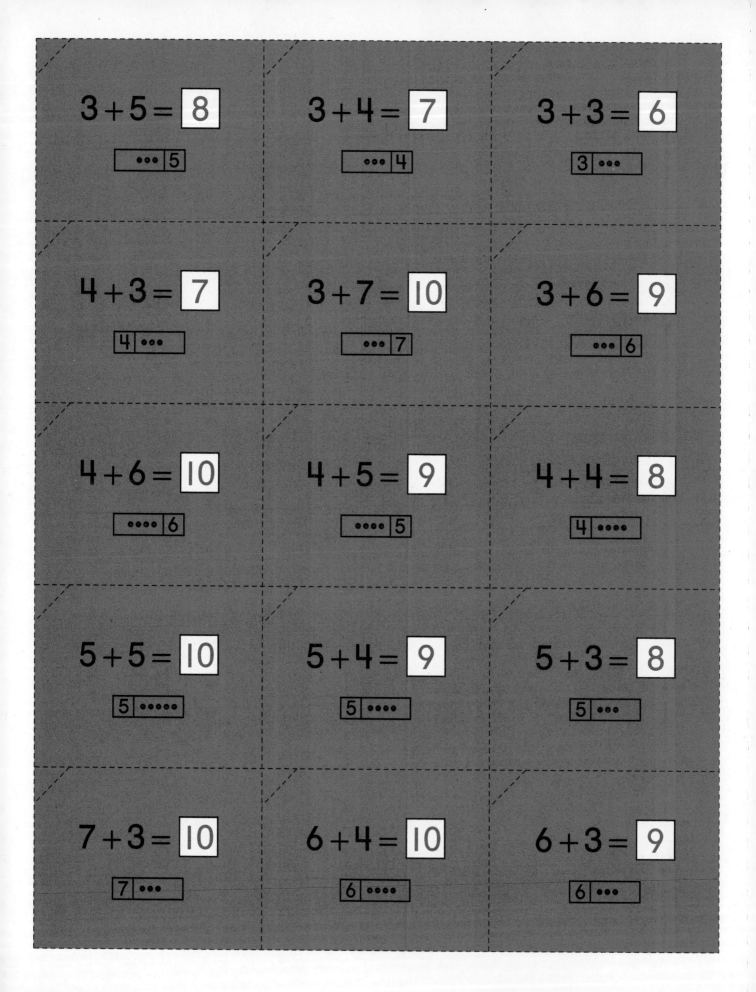

3 + 5 = 8

3 + 4 = 7

3 + 3 = 6

4 + 3 = 7

3 + 7 = 10

3 + 6 = 9

4 + 6 = 10

4 + 5 = 9

4 + 4 = 8

5 + 5 = 10

5 + 4 = 9

5 + 3 = 8

7 + 3 = 10

6 + 4 = 10

6 + 3 = 9

Red Count-On Cards

Number Quilt 1: Unknown Totals

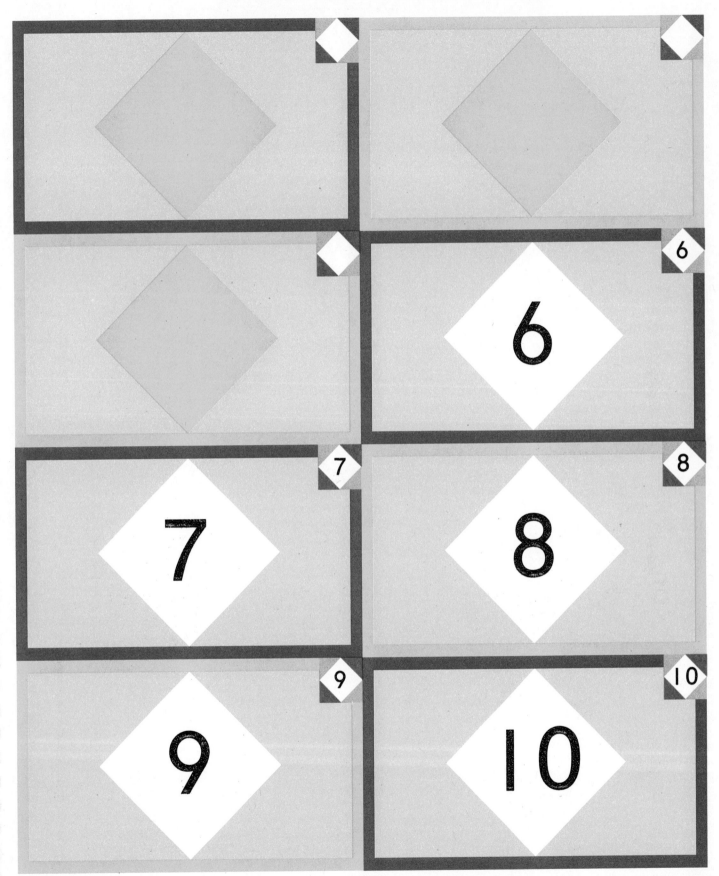

Use with the Red Count-On Cards.

Name _____

Draw more to count on. Write how many in all.

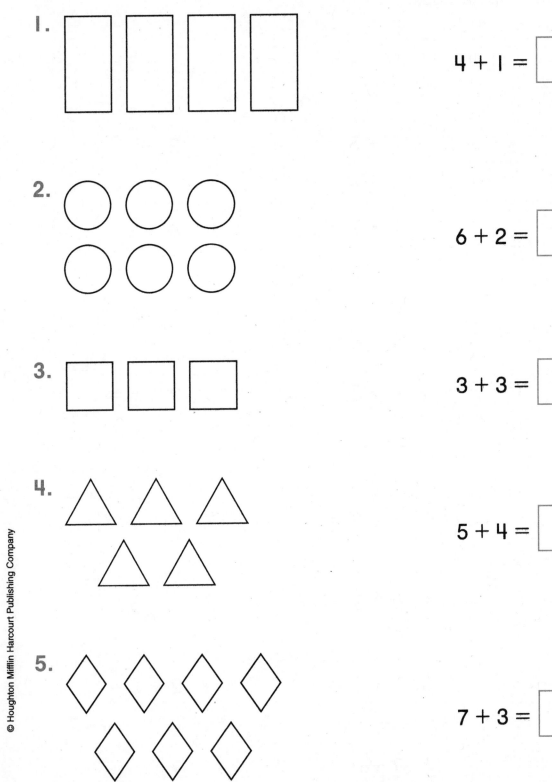

1. $4 + 1 = \boxed{}$

2. $6 + 2 = \boxed{}$

3. $3 + 3 = \boxed{}$

4. $5 + 4 = \boxed{}$

5. $7 + 3 = \boxed{}$

Name

Underline the greater number.
Count on from that number.

6. 2 + <u>8</u> = ☐   7. 5 + 4 = ☐   8. 6 + 3 = ☐

9. 7 + 3 = ☐   10. 2 + 5 = ☐   11. 3 + 4 = ☐

12. 4 + 3 = ☐   13. 2 + 7 = ☐   14. 8 + 2 = ☐

15. 3 + 6 = ☐   16. 5 + 2 = ☐   17. 6 + 2 = ☐

18. 5 + 3 = ☐   19. 4 + 5 = ☐   20. 2 + 6 = ☐

PATH to FLUENCY Add.

1. 3 + 2 = ☐   2. 1 + 9 = ☐   3. 7 + 0 = ☐

4. 8 + 1 = ☐   5. 0 + 9 = ☐   6. 1 + 6 = ☐

7. 8 + 0 = ☐   8. 7 + 1 = ☐   9. 2 + 3 = ☐

10. 0 + 10 = ☐   11. 9 + 0 = ☐   12. 9 + 1 = ☐

Addition Games: Unknown Totals

Name _____

Solve. Write how many are left.

1.   There are 8 apples.

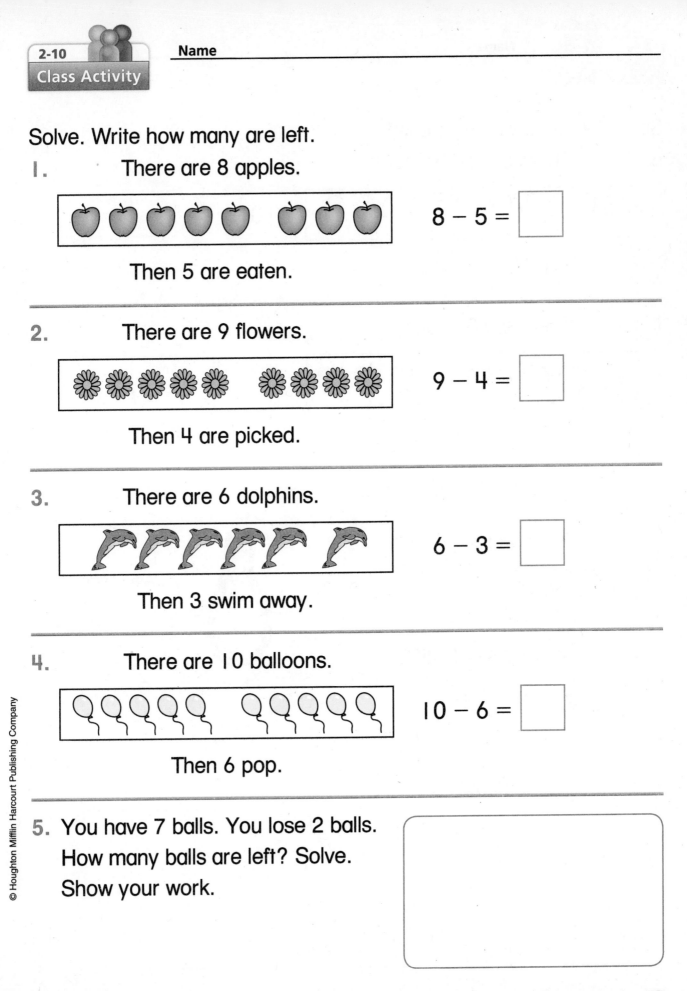

Then 5 are eaten.

$8 - 5 =$ ☐

2.   There are 9 flowers.

Then 4 are picked.

$9 - 4 =$ ☐

3.   There are 6 dolphins.

Then 3 swim away.

$6 - 3 =$ ☐

4.   There are 10 balloons.

Then 6 pop.

$10 - 6 =$ ☐

5. You have 7 balls. You lose 2 balls.
How many balls are left? Solve.
Show your work.

Solve. Write how many are left.

6. There are 10 balloons.

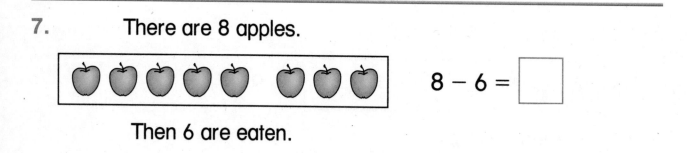

$10 - 4 = \boxed{}$

Then 4 pop.

7. There are 8 apples.

$8 - 6 = \boxed{}$

Then 6 are eaten.

8. Look at Puzzled Penguin's work.

There were 7 flowers.

Then 3 were picked.

$7 - 3 = \boxed{3}$

Am I correct?

9. Help Puzzled Penguin.

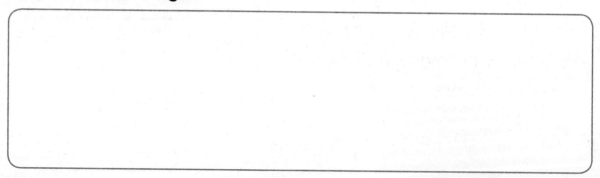

Represent Subtraction

Subtract and write the equation.

1.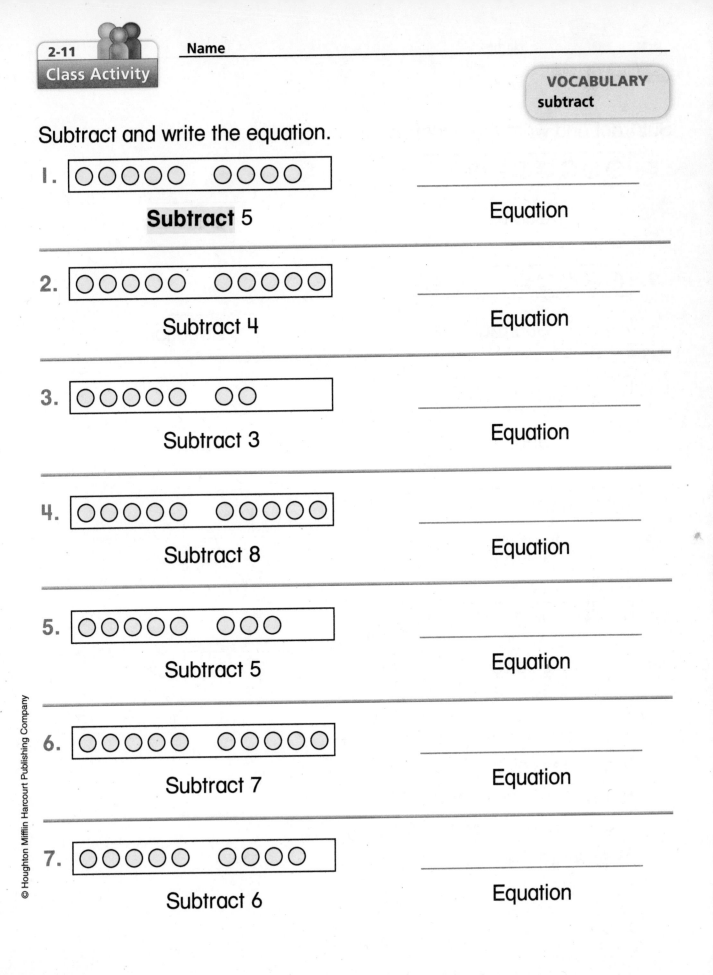

Subtract 5

_____
Equation

2.

Subtract 4

_____
Equation

3.

Subtract 3

_____
Equation

4.

Subtract 8

_____
Equation

5.

Subtract 5

_____
Equation

6.

Subtract 7

_____
Equation

7.

Subtract 6

_____
Equation

Subtract and write the equation.

8. ⊙⊙⊙⊙⊙ ⊙⊙⊙

Subtract 5   _____
                            Equation

9. ⊙⊙⊙⊙⊙ ⊙⊙⊙⊙

Subtract 3   _____
                            Equation

10. ⊙⊙⊙⊙⊙ ⊙⊙⊙⊙⊙

Subtract 6   _____
                            Equation

11. ⊙⊙⊙⊙⊙ ⊙⊙

Subtract 4   _____
                            Equation

12. ⊙⊙⊙⊙⊙ ⊙⊙⊙⊙

Subtract 2   _____
                            Equation

13. There are 6 marbles on the table.
    4 marbles roll off. How many
    marbles are there now?
    Use a circle drawing to solve.
    Then write the equation.

Subtraction with Drawings and Equations

Name _____

Use the picture to solve the equation.

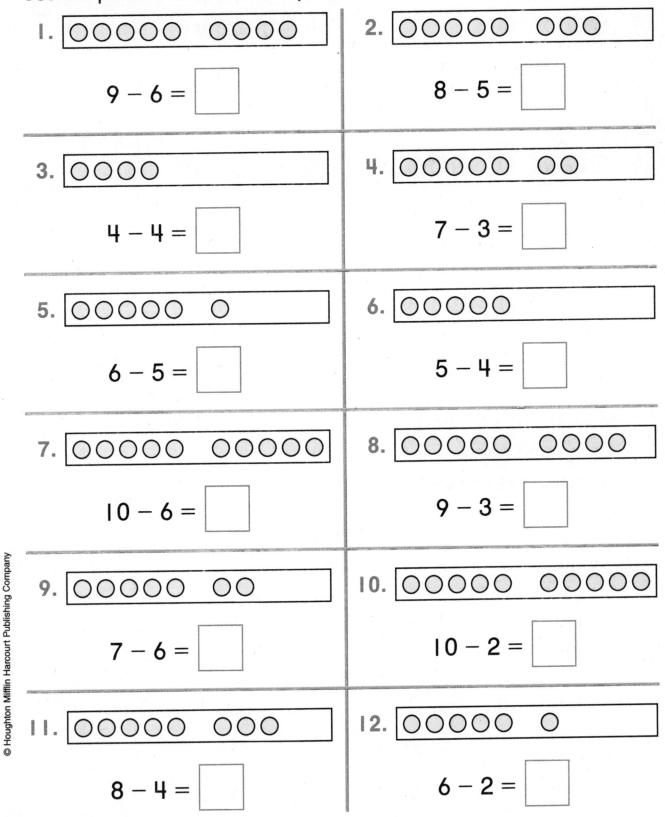

1. $9 - 6 = \boxed{}$

2. $8 - 5 = \boxed{}$

3. $4 - 4 = \boxed{}$

4. $7 - 3 = \boxed{}$

5. $6 - 5 = \boxed{}$

6. $5 - 4 = \boxed{}$

7. $10 - 6 = \boxed{}$

8. $9 - 3 = \boxed{}$

9. $7 - 6 = \boxed{}$

10. $10 - 2 = \boxed{}$

11. $8 - 4 = \boxed{}$

12. $6 - 2 = \boxed{}$

Name _____

Use the picture to solve the equation.

13. ⃝⃝⃝⃝⃝

$5 - 3 = \boxed{}$

14. ⃝⃝⃝⃝⃝ ⃝⃝

$7 - 4 = \boxed{}$

15. ⃝⃝⃝⃝⃝ ⃝⃝⃝⃝

$9 - 5 = \boxed{}$

16. ⃝⃝⃝⃝⃝ ⃝

$6 - 4 = \boxed{}$

17. ⃝⃝⃝⃝⃝ ⃝⃝⃝⃝⃝

$10 - 3 = \boxed{}$

18. ⃝⃝⃝⃝⃝ ⃝⃝⃝

$8 - 6 = \boxed{}$

19. Make a circle drawing
for the equation $6 - 2 = \boxed{}$.
Then find the answer.

PATH to
FLUENCY Subtract.

1. $2 - 1 = \boxed{}$ 2. $6 - 0 = \boxed{}$ 3. $1 - 0 = \boxed{}$

4. $4 - 1 = \boxed{}$ 5. $3 - 1 = \boxed{}$ 6. $10 - 0 = \boxed{}$

7. $8 - 1 = \boxed{}$ 8. $5 - 0 = \boxed{}$ 9. $5 - 1 = \boxed{}$

Practice with Subtraction

Relate addition and subtraction.

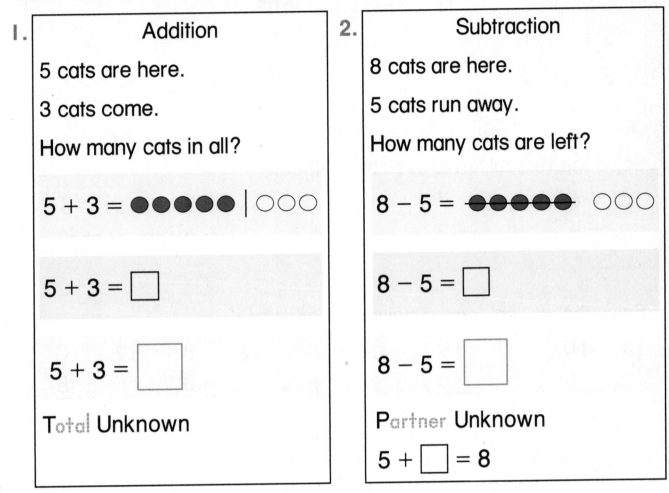

1. | **Addition**
5 cats are here.

3 cats come.

How many cats in all?

$5 + 3 = $ ●●●●● | ○○○

$5 + 3 = \square$

$5 + 3 = \square$

Total Unknown

2. | **Subtraction**
8 cats are here.

5 cats run away.

How many cats are left?

$8 - 5 = $ ●●●●● ○○○

$8 - 5 = \square$

$8 - 5 = \square$

Partner Unknown

$5 + \square = 8$

Use addition to solve subtraction.

3. $4 + 4 = 8$, so I know $8 - 4 = \square$.

4. $6 + 3 = 9$, so I know $9 - 6 = \square$.

5. $7 + 3 = 10$, so I know $10 - 7 = \square$.

6. $5 + 4 = 9$, so I know $9 - 5 = \square$.

7. $3 + 3 = 6$, so I know $6 - 3 = \square$.

VOCABULARY
vertical forms

Equations	Vertical Forms	
$5 + 3 = 8$	5	8
$8 - 5 = 3$	$+ 3$	$- 5$
	8	3

Solve the vertical form. Use any method.

8. 6
  $+ 4$

9. 7
  $+ 2$

10. 1
  $+ 6$

11. 2
  $+ 6$

12. 3
  $+ 7$

Solve the vertical form. Think about addition.

13. 10
  $- 8$

14. 9
  $- 5$

15. 7
  $- 1$

16. 8
  $- 3$

17. 10
  $- 5$

PATH to FLUENCY Subtract.

1. $4 - 0 = \boxed{}$

2. $6 - 1 = \boxed{}$

3. $4 - 2 = \boxed{}$

4. $9 - 1 = \boxed{}$

5. $5 - 2 = \boxed{}$

6. $8 - 0 = \boxed{}$

7. $3 - 2 = \boxed{}$

8. $9 - 0 = \boxed{}$

9. $7 - 1 = \boxed{}$

10. $6 - 0 = \boxed{}$

11. $8 - 1 = \boxed{}$

12. $10 - 0 = \boxed{}$

► **Math and the Animal Park**

Darya and her family go to the animal park.

Use the picture to solve the equation.

1. Darya sees 5 lions. Then she sees 3 more lions.

How many lions does she see in all? $5 + 3 = \boxed{}$

2. Nick sees 9 crocodiles in the water.

Then 2 crocodiles climb out.

How many crocodiles are in the water now? $9 - 2 = \boxed{}$

Name

Use the picture to solve the equation.

3. Ray sees 1 cheetah in a tree and 7 lions under a tree.

How many wild cats does he see?   1 + 7 = ☐

4. Sophie sees 8 baboons and 2 mandrills.

How many monkeys does she see?   8 + 2 = ☐

Focus on Mathematical Practices

Write the partners and the total.

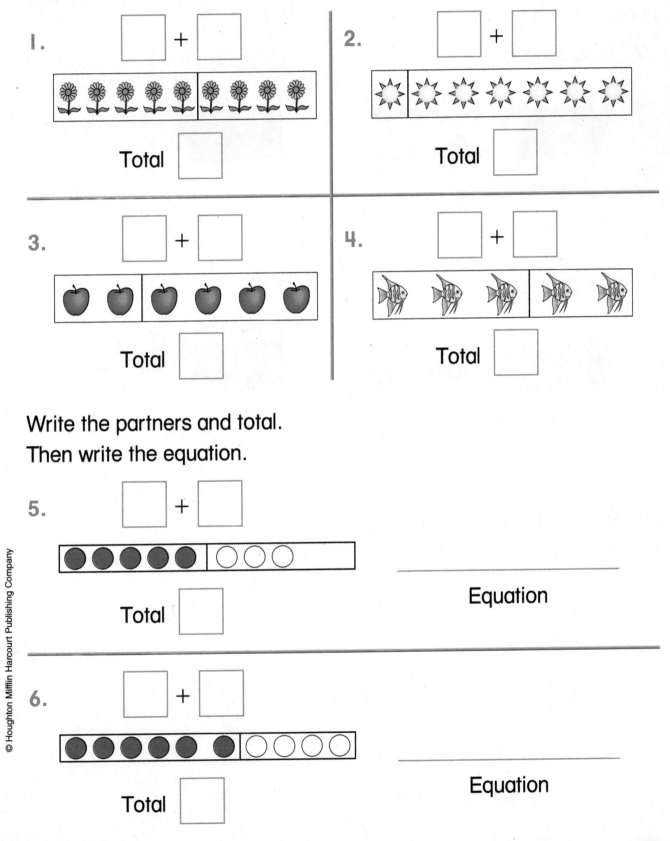

1. ☐ + ☐

    Total ☐

2. ☐ + ☐

    Total ☐

3. ☐ + ☐

    Total ☐

4. ☐ + ☐

    Total ☐

Write the partners and total.
Then write the equation.

5. ☐ + ☐

    Total ☐

    _____
    Equation

6. ☐ + ☐

    Total ☐

    _____
    Equation

Find the total number of toys
in each group.

7. 5 cars in the box

☐ Total

8. 6 boats in the box

☐ Total

9. 8 dolls in the box

☐ Total

10. 3 balls in the box

☐ Total

Underline the greater number.
Count on from that number.

11. $3 + 7 =$ ☐   12. $5 + 4 =$ ☐   13. $6 + 2 =$ ☐

14. $4 + 6 =$ ☐   15. $8 + 2 =$ ☐   16. $3 + 4 =$ ☐

Write how many are left.
Use the picture to help you.

17. There are 10 crayons.

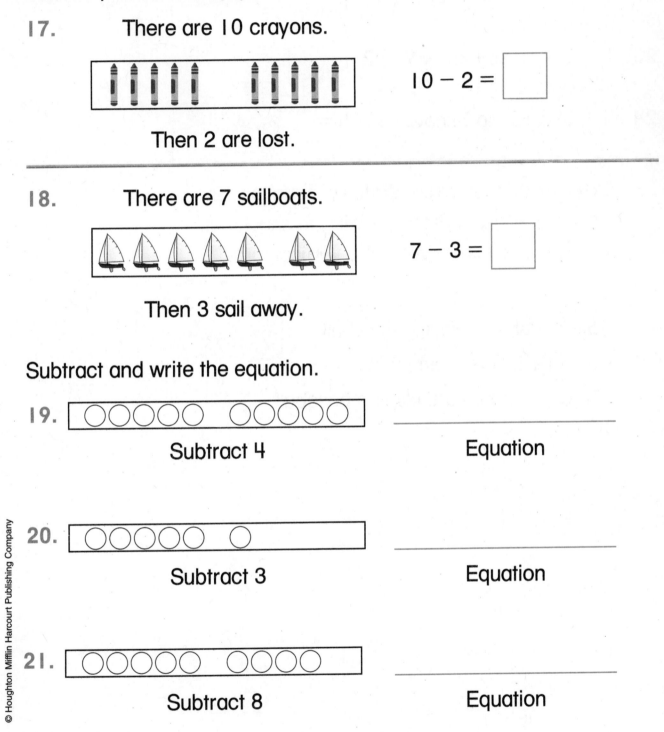

$10 - 2 = \boxed{}$

Then 2 are lost.

18. There are 7 sailboats.

$7 - 3 = \boxed{}$

Then 3 sail away.

Subtract and write the equation.

19.

Subtract 4

_____
Equation

20.

Subtract 3

_____
Equation

21.

Subtract 8

_____
Equation

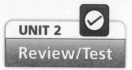

Name _____

Use addition to solve subtraction.

22. $6 + 4 = 10$, so I know $10 - 4 = \boxed{}$.

23. $7 + 2 = 9$, so I know $9 - 2 = \boxed{}$.

24. $5 + 5 = 10$, so I know $10 - 5 = \boxed{}$.

---

25. **Extended Response** Write an equation for the story. Make a Proof Drawing to show that the equation is true. Write the vertical form.

> 6 children are playing baseball.
>
> 3 more children join them.
>
> Now 9 children are playing baseball.

Family Letter

Dear Family:

Your child has started a new unit on story problems. Because most children this age are learning to read, your child may need help reading the story problems. Offer help when it is needed, but do not give the answer.

To solve story problems, children first need to know which number is unknown. Is it the total or one of the parts? This program helps children focus on this important issue by using "Math Mountains." In a Math Mountain, the total sits at the top and the parts (or partners) sit at the bottom of the mountain. Children can quickly see the relationship between the partners and the total when they look at the mountain.

Math Mountain

Math Mountains are especially helpful in showing children how to find an unknown partner, as in the following problem: *I see 9 horses. 5 are black, and the others are white. How many horses are white?*

Children can find the answer by drawing the mountain to see which number is unknown. Then they count on from the partner they know to the total. In this way, they can find the partner they don't know.

Math Mountain with
Unknown Partner

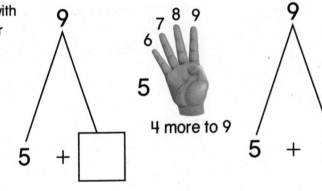

4 more to 9

If you have any questions, please contact me.

Sincerely,
Your child's teacher

COMMON CORE

This unit includes the Common Core Standards for Mathematical Content for Operations and Algebraic Thinking, 1.OA.1, 1.OA.4, 1.OA.5, 1.OA.6, 1.OA.8 and all Mathematical Practices.

Estimada familia:

Su niño ha empezado una nueva unidad donde aprenderá cómo resolver problemas matemáticos. Como la mayoría de los niños a esta edad aún están aprendiendo a leer, es probable que su niño necesite ayuda para leer los problemas. Ofrezca ayuda cuando haga falta, pero no dé la respuesta.

Para resolver problemas, los niños primero deben hallar el número desconocido. ¿Es el total o una de las partes? Este programa los ayuda a concentrarse en este punto importante usando "Montañas matemáticas". En una montaña matemática el total está en la cima y las partes están al pie de la montaña. Al ver la montaña, los niños pueden ver rápidamente la relación entre las partes y el total.

Montaña
matemática

Las montañas matemáticas son especialmente útiles para mostrar a los niños cómo hallar una parte desconocida, como en el problema siguiente: *Veo 9 caballos. 5 son negros y los demás son blancos. ¿Cuántos caballos son blancos?*

Los niños pueden hallar la respuesta dibujando la montaña para saber cuál es el número desconocido. Luego, cuentan hacia adelante a partir de la parte que conocen para hallar el total. De esta manera, pueden hallar la parte desconocida.

Montaña matemática
con parte
desconocida

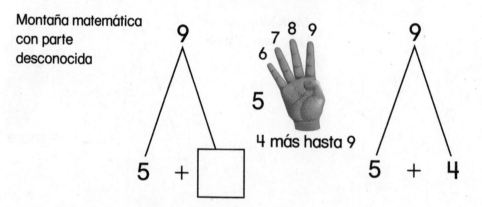

4 más hasta 9

Si tiene alguna pregunta, por favor comuníquese conmigo.

Atentamente,
El maestro de su niño

Esta unidad incluye los Common Core Standards for Mathematical Content for Operations and Algebraic Thinking, 1.OA.1, 1.OA.4, 1.OA.5, 1.OA.6, 1.OA.8 and all Mathematical Practices.

Explore Unknowns

Find the **unknown partner**.

1.

6

4 + ☐

2.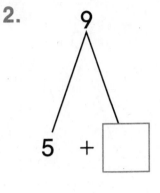

9

5 + ☐

3.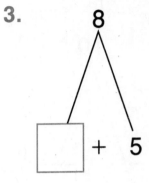

8

☐ + 5

4.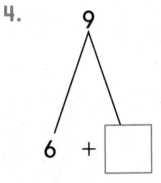

9

6 + ☐

5.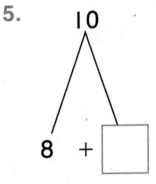

10

8 + ☐

6.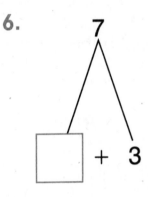

7

☐ + 3

7.

10

5 + ☐

8.

8

☐ + 6

9.

6

3 + ☐

10.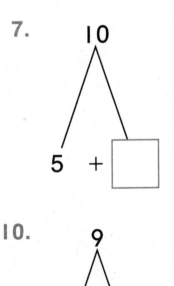

9

4 + ☐

11.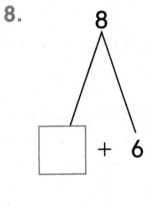

5

☐ + 2

12.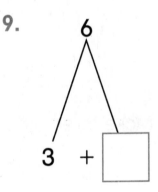

7

2 + ☐

13. Make three different Math Mountains with a total of 10.

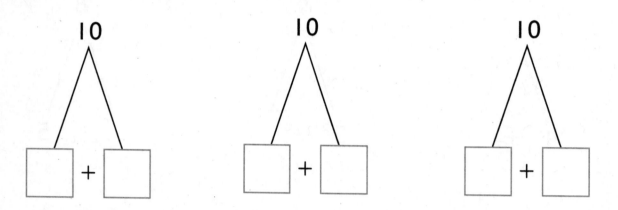

14. Make three different Math Mountains with a total of 8.

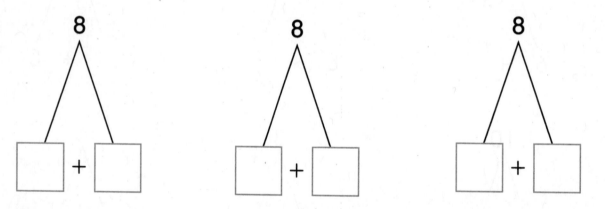

15. Make three different Math Mountains with a total of 7.

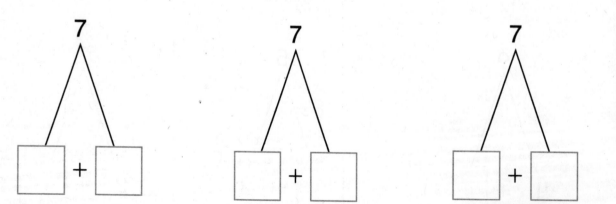

Explore Unknowns

3-2 Class Activity

Name ____________________

VOCABULARY
story problem
label

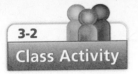

Solve the **story problem**.

Show your work. Use drawings, numbers, or words.

---

1. We see 9 fish.
5 are big. The others are small.
How many fish are small?

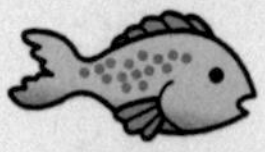

fish

☐ ____________________
label

---

2. 8 boys are riding bikes.
6 ride fast. The rest ride slow.
How many boys ride slow?

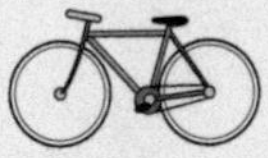

bike

☐ ____________________
label

---

3. Ana has 2 hats.
Then she gets more.
Now she has 5.
How many hats does she get?

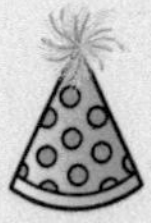

hat

☐ ____________________
label

---

4. Discuss why it is important to write a **label** in the answer.

Solve the story problem. Use cubes to help.

5. Raja has 6 plums. He wants to put some on each of two plates. How many can he put on each plate? Show 4 answers.

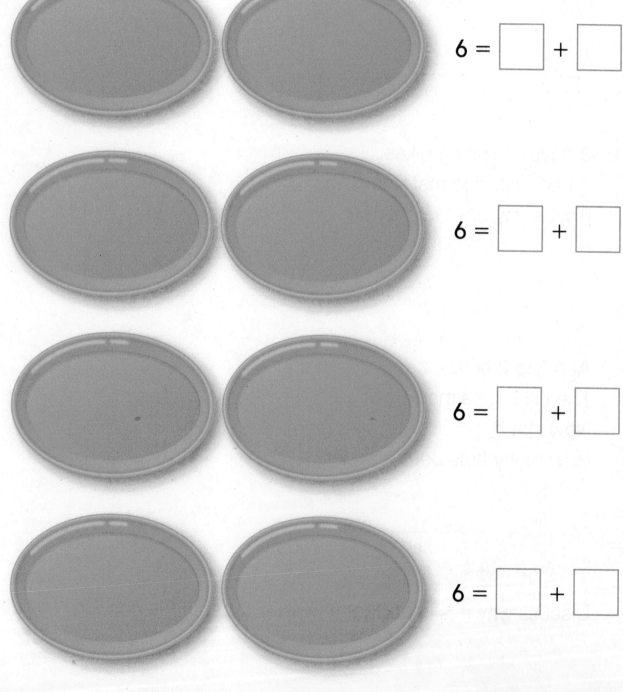

$6 = \boxed{} + \boxed{}$

$6 = \boxed{} + \boxed{}$

$6 = \boxed{} + \boxed{}$

$6 = \boxed{} + \boxed{}$

Count on to find the unknown partner.

1. $3 +$ $\boxed{}$ $= 6$ 2. $7 +$ $\boxed{}$ $= 10$ 3. $2 +$ $\boxed{}$ $= 6$

4. $7 +$ $\boxed{}$ $= 9$ 5. $4 +$ $\boxed{}$ $= 8$ 6. $5 +$ $\boxed{}$ $= 8$

Count on to solve.

7. 6 letters total

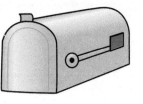

How many letters
are in the box? $\boxed{}$ _____
                              label

8. 10 footprints total

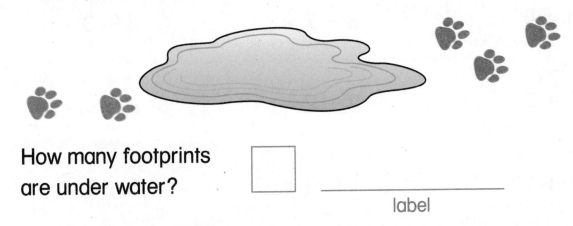

How many footprints
are under water? $\boxed{}$ _____
                              label

9. Look at Puzzled Penguin's work.

$2 + \boxed{} = 8$

$2 + \boxed{10} = 8$

Am I correct?

10. Help Puzzled Penguin.

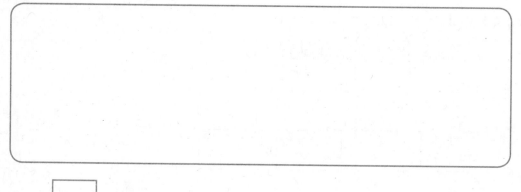

$2 + \boxed{} = 8$

PATH to FLUENCY Add.

1. $4 + 4 = \boxed{}$ 2. $3 + 7 = \boxed{}$ 3. $3 + 3 = \boxed{}$

4. $8 + 2 = \boxed{}$ 5. $2 + 2 = \boxed{}$ 6. $6 + 4 = \boxed{}$

7. $1 + 1 = \boxed{}$ 8. $1 + 9 = \boxed{}$ 9. $5 + 5 = \boxed{}$

10. $7 + 3 = \boxed{}$ 11. $2 + 8 = \boxed{}$ 12. $4 + 6 = \boxed{}$

Solve Equations with Unknown Partners

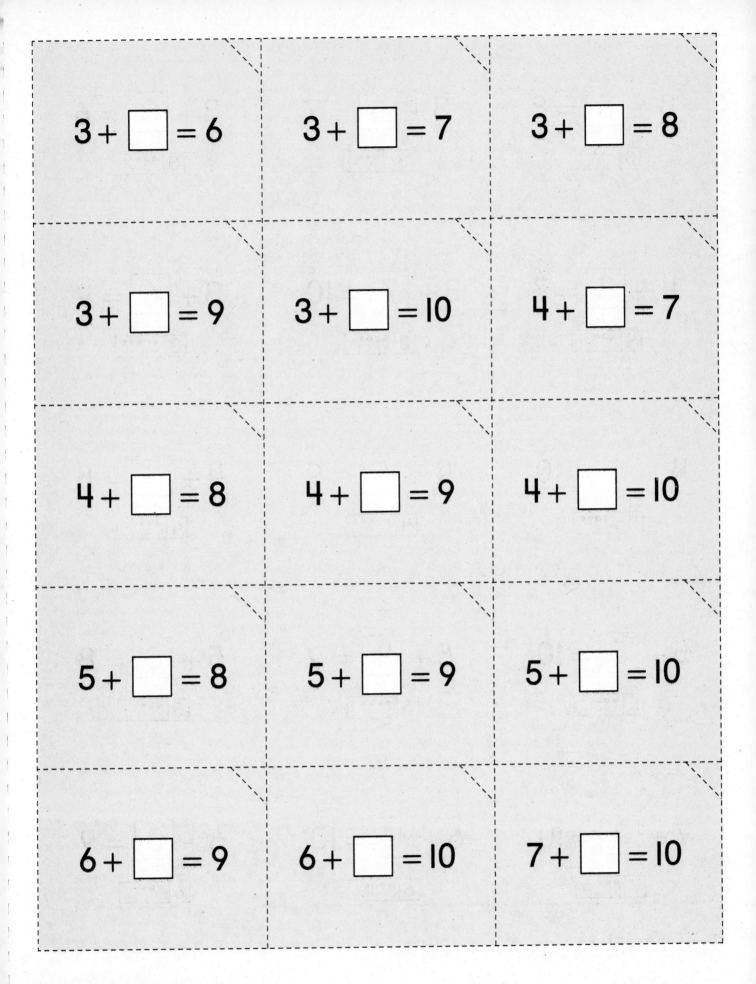

$3 + \boxed{} = 6$

$3 + \boxed{} = 7$

$3 + \boxed{} = 8$

$3 + \boxed{} = 9$

$3 + \boxed{} = 10$

$4 + \boxed{} = 7$

$4 + \boxed{} = 8$

$4 + \boxed{} = 9$

$4 + \boxed{} = 10$

$5 + \boxed{} = 8$

$5 + \boxed{} = 9$

$5 + \boxed{} = 10$

$6 + \boxed{} = 9$

$6 + \boxed{} = 10$

$7 + \boxed{} = 10$

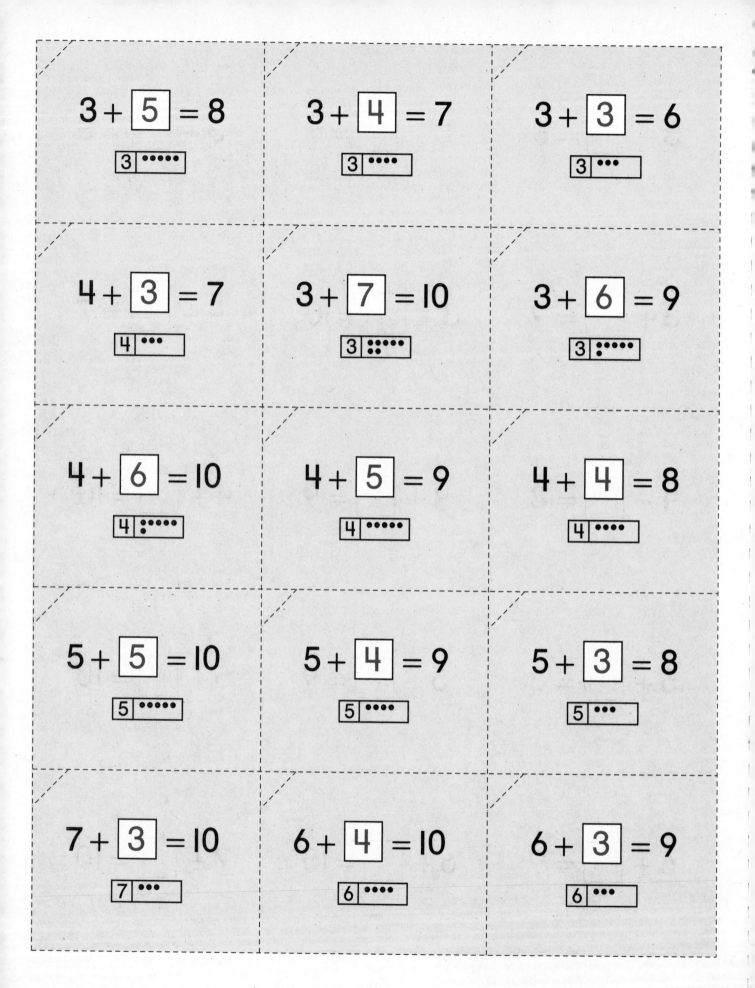

$3 + \boxed{5} = 8$

$3 + \boxed{4} = 7$

$3 + \boxed{3} = 6$

$4 + \boxed{3} = 7$

$3 + \boxed{7} = 10$

$3 + \boxed{6} = 9$

$4 + \boxed{6} = 10$

$4 + \boxed{5} = 9$

$4 + \boxed{4} = 8$

$5 + \boxed{5} = 10$

$5 + \boxed{4} = 9$

$5 + \boxed{3} = 8$

$7 + \boxed{3} = 10$

$6 + \boxed{4} = 10$

$6 + \boxed{3} = 9$

Yellow Count-On Cards

Number Quilt 2: Unknown Partners

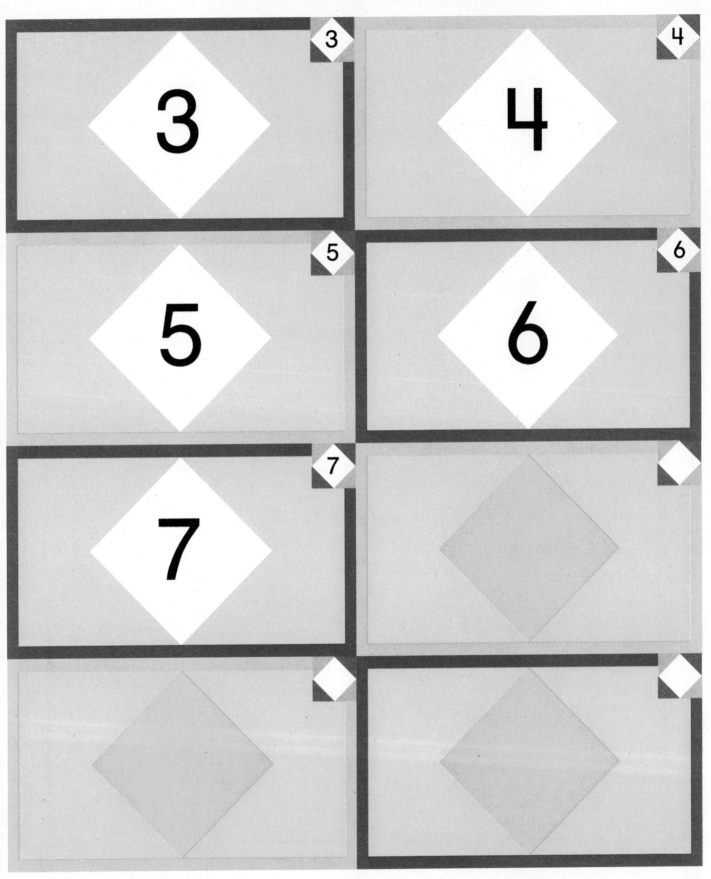

UNIT 3 LESSON 4
© Houghton Mifflin Harcourt Publishing Company

Number Quilt 2 **73**
Use with the Yellow or Orange Count-On Cards.

Solve the story problem.

Show your work. Use drawings, numbers, or words.

1. Sam has 4 balloons.
   Then he gets some more.
   Now he has 9.
   How many balloons does he get?

   ☐ _____
         label

   balloon

2. There are 8 crayons on the table.
   5 are red.
   The others are green.
   How many crayons are green?

   ☐ _____
         label

   table

3. Rabia sees 10 eagles.
   3 are in a tree.
   The rest are flying.
   How many eagles are flying?

   ☐ _____
         label

   eagle

Solve the story problem.

Show your work. Use drawings, numbers, or words.

---

4. Maddox has 3 toy trains.
   Then he gets more.
   Now he has 7.
   How many trains does he get?

   ☐ _____
       label

train

---

5. We pick 10 apples from the trees.
   6 are green. Some are red.
   How many apples are red?

   ☐ _____
       label

tree

---

6. Milena wants to put 8 balls
   in a box. She wants to have
   soccer balls and footballs.
   How many of each ball could
   she use? Show three answers.

soccer ball

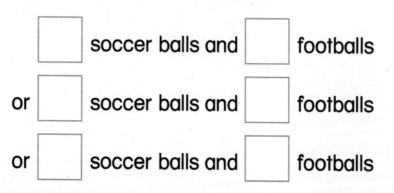

☐ soccer balls and ☐ footballs

or ☐ soccer balls and ☐ footballs

or ☐ soccer balls and ☐ footballs

Addition Game: Unknown Partners

VOCABULARY
subtraction story problem

Solve the **subtraction story problem**. Show your work. Use drawings, numbers, or words.

1. 8 flies are on a log.
   6 are eaten by a frog.
   How many flies are left?

   ☐ _____
      label

   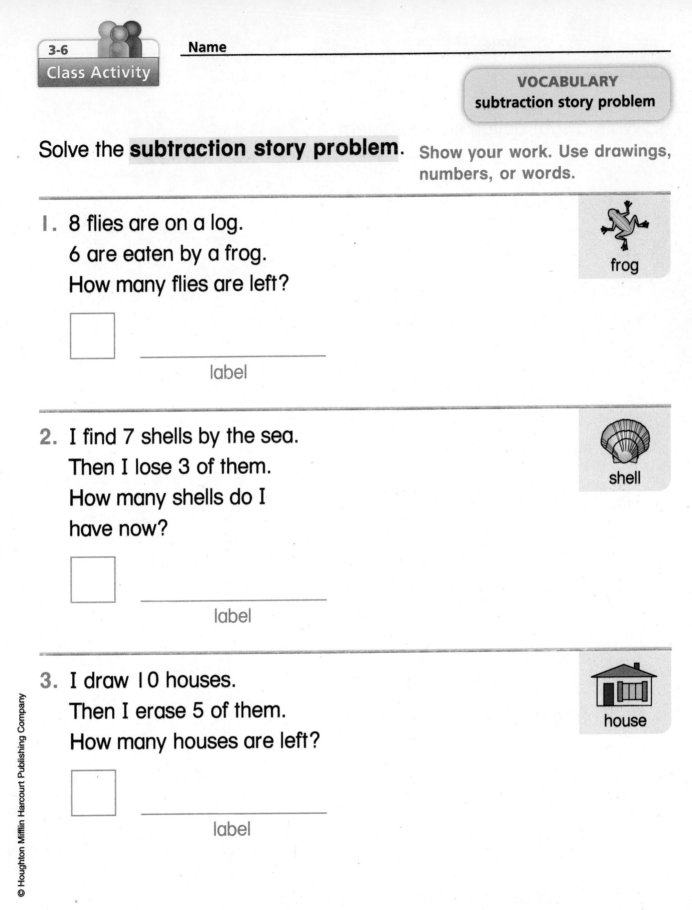

   frog

2. I find 7 shells by the sea.
   Then I lose 3 of them.
   How many shells do I
   have now?

   ☐ _____
      label

   shell

3. I draw 10 houses.
   Then I erase 5 of them.
   How many houses are left?

   ☐ _____
      label

   house

Name _____

4. Write a subtraction story problem.

_____

- -

_____

_____

- -

_____

_____

- -

_____

5. Write an equation to solve.

Use a box for the unknown number.

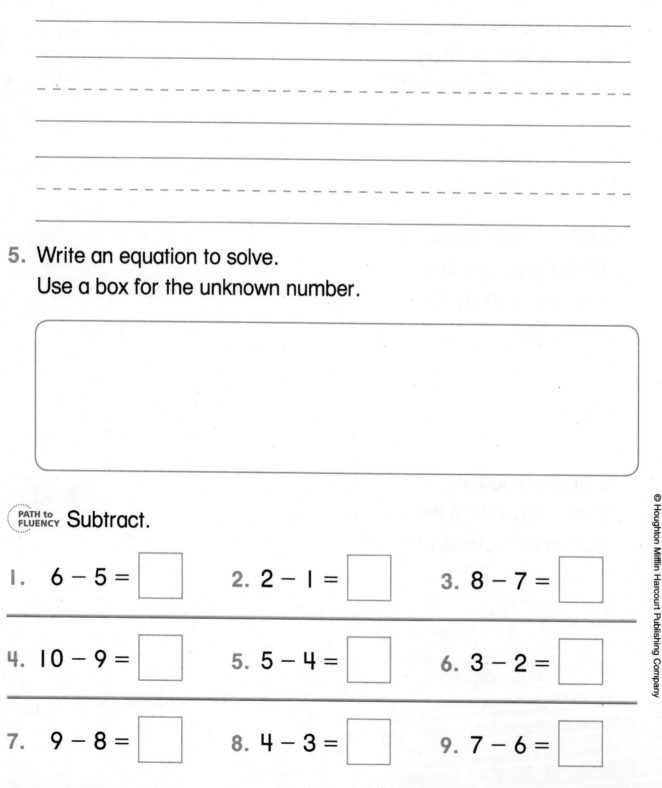

PATH to FLUENCY Subtract.

1. $6 - 5 = \boxed{}$ 2. $2 - 1 = \boxed{}$ 3. $8 - 7 = \boxed{}$

4. $10 - 9 = \boxed{}$ 5. $5 - 4 = \boxed{}$ 6. $3 - 2 = \boxed{}$

7. $9 - 8 = \boxed{}$ 8. $4 - 3 = \boxed{}$ 9. $7 - 6 = \boxed{}$

Subtraction Strategies

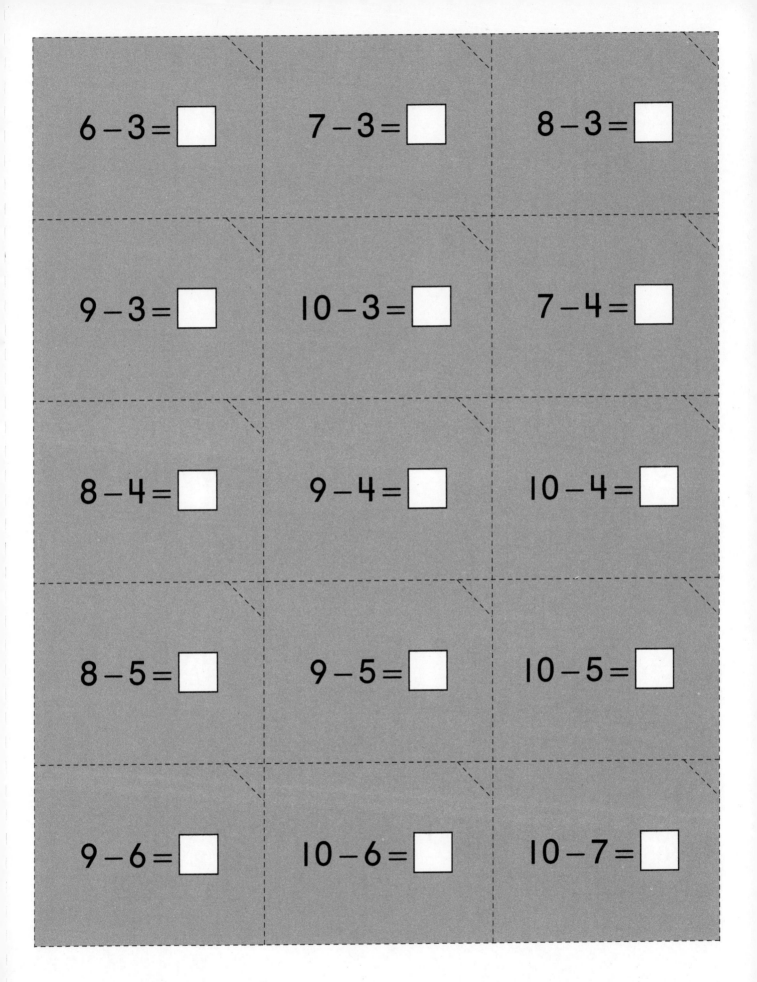

$6 - 3 = \boxed{}$

$7 - 3 = \boxed{}$

$8 - 3 = \boxed{}$

$9 - 3 = \boxed{}$

$10 - 3 = \boxed{}$

$7 - 4 = \boxed{}$

$8 - 4 = \boxed{}$

$9 - 4 = \boxed{}$

$10 - 4 = \boxed{}$

$8 - 5 = \boxed{}$

$9 - 5 = \boxed{}$

$10 - 5 = \boxed{}$

$9 - 6 = \boxed{}$

$10 - 6 = \boxed{}$

$10 - 7 = \boxed{}$

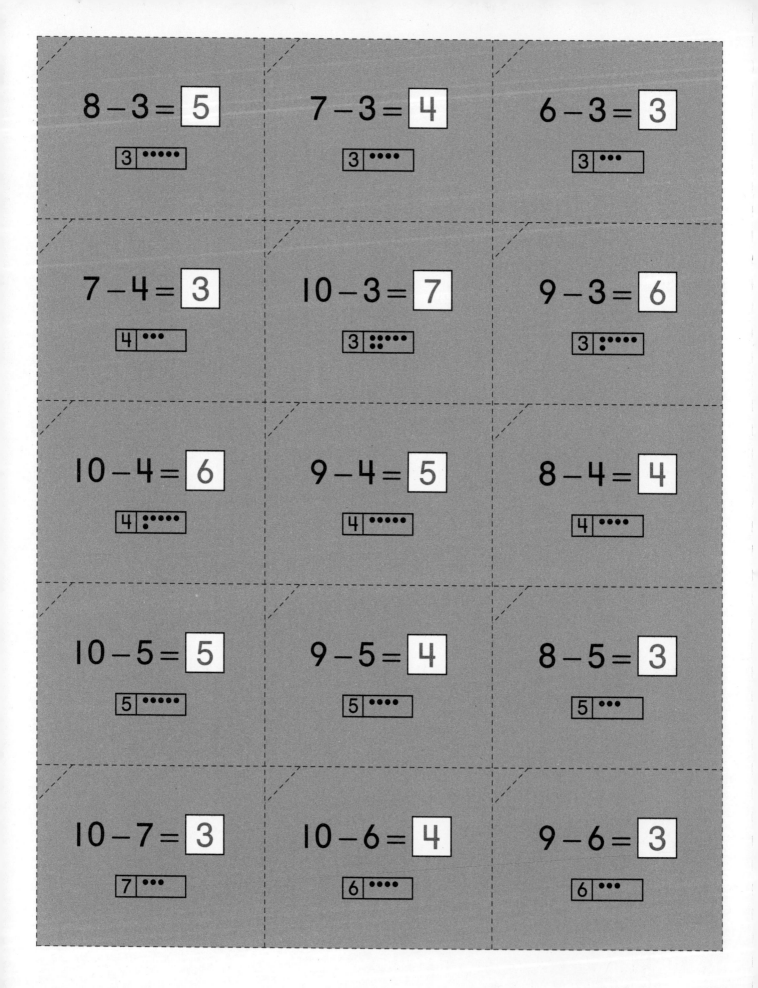

$8 - 3 = \boxed{5}$

$7 - 3 = \boxed{4}$

$6 - 3 = \boxed{3}$

$7 - 4 = \boxed{3}$

$10 - 3 = \boxed{7}$

$9 - 3 = \boxed{6}$

$10 - 4 = \boxed{6}$

$9 - 4 = \boxed{5}$

$8 - 4 = \boxed{4}$

$10 - 5 = \boxed{5}$

$9 - 5 = \boxed{4}$

$8 - 5 = \boxed{3}$

$10 - 7 = \boxed{3}$

$10 - 6 = \boxed{4}$

$9 - 6 = \boxed{3}$

Orange Count-On Cards

Solve and discuss.

1. We see 10 dogs.

7 run away.

How many are left?

   [ ]   _____
              label

2. We see 9 dogs.

5 are not barking.

The rest are barking.

How many are barking?

   [ ]   _____
              label

3. **Discuss** How are the methods you used to solve the problems alike and different?

Solve the story problem.

Show your work. Use drawings, numbers, or words.

4. There are 8 apples. 6 apples are eaten.
   How many apples are there now?

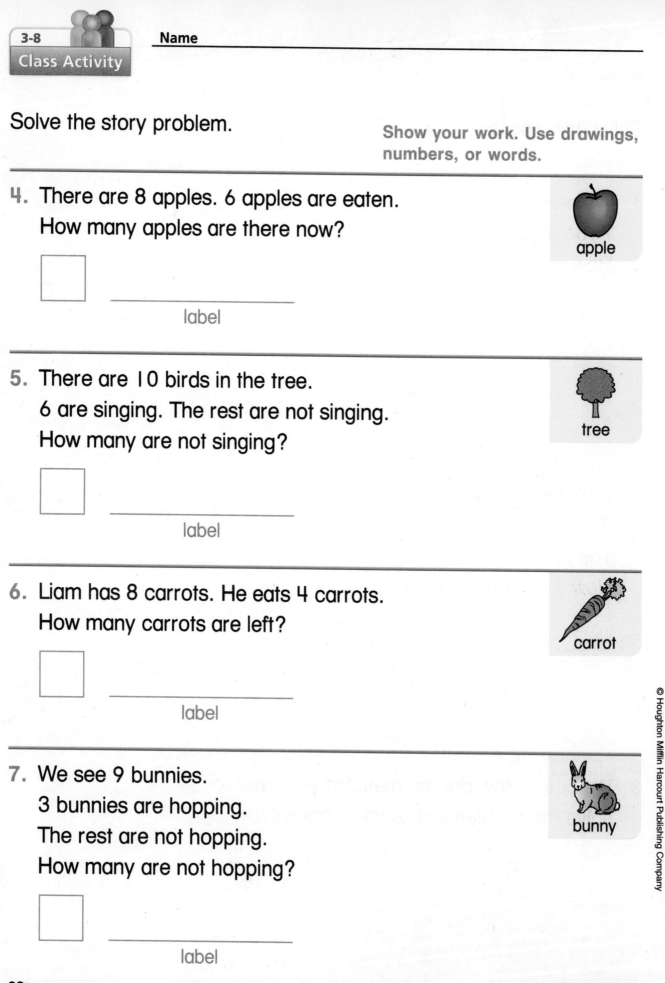

apple

   ☐ _____
      label

5. There are 10 birds in the tree.
   6 are singing. The rest are not singing.
   How many are not singing?

tree

   ☐ _____
      label

6. Liam has 8 carrots. He eats 4 carrots.
   How many carrots are left?

carrot

   ☐ _____
      label

7. We see 9 bunnies.
   3 bunnies are hopping.
   The rest are not hopping.
   How many are not hopping?

bunny

   ☐ _____
      label

Practice with Subtraction Stories

Solve and discuss.

1. There are 4 cats.
   3 more cats join them.
   How many cats are there now?

   $4 + 3 =$ ⬜

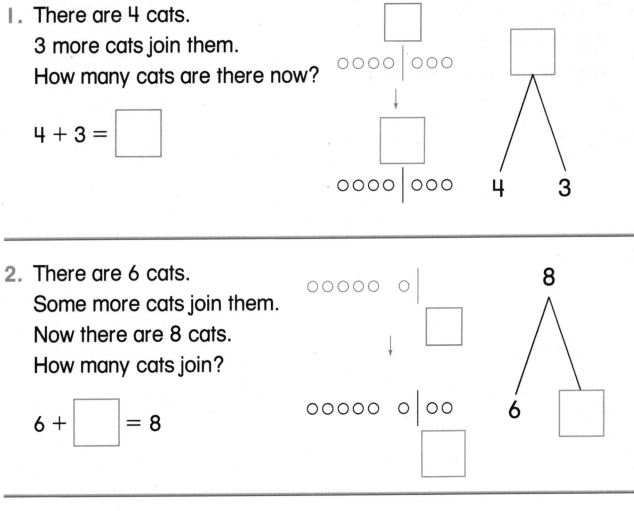

2. There are 6 cats.
   Some more cats join them.
   Now there are 8 cats.
   How many cats join?

   $6 +$ ⬜ $= 8$

3. There are some cats.
   4 more cats join them.
   Now there are 9 cats.
   How many cats are there
   at the start?

   ⬜ $+ 4 = 9$

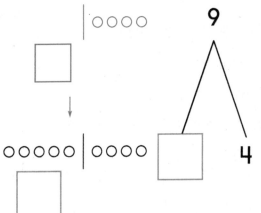

Solve and discuss.

4. There are 7 cats.
   3 cats walk away.
   How many cats are left?

   $7 - 3 = \boxed{}$

   $3 + \boxed{} = 7$

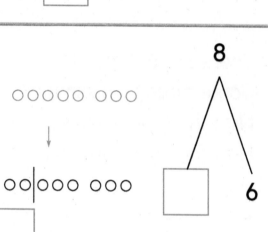

5. There are 8 cats.
   Some cats walk away.
   There are 6 cats left.
   How many cats walk away?

   $8 - \boxed{} = 6$

   $6 + \boxed{} = 8$

6. There are some cats.
   4 cats walk away.
   Now there are 5 cats.
   How many cats are there
   at the start?

   $\boxed{} - 4 = 5$

   $5 + 4 = \boxed{}$

Relate Addition and Subtraction Situations

Solve the story problem.

Show your work. Use drawings, numbers, or words.

7. 10 kittens are in the bed. 7 are
    not sleeping. The rest are sleeping.
    How many are sleeping?

    [3] K i t t e n s
    _____
    label

    $10 - 7 = 3$

    kitten

8. Emma has 5 beads. She gets some more
    beads. Now she has 9 beads. How many
    beads does she get?

    [4] beads
    _____
    label

    $5 + \square \; 9$

    bead

9. 8 boys are at the park. Some boys go home.
    3 boys are left. How many boys go home?

    [9] boys
    _____
    label

    $8 - \square \; 3$

    boy

10. Some horses are in the barn. 3 more horses
    go in. 7 horses are in the barn now.
    How many are there at the start?

    [4] horses
    _____
    label

    $\boxed{4} + 3 = 7$

    barn

Solve the story problem.

11. Dad picks some flowers. He puts 2 in the red vase and the other 5 in the blue vase. How many does he pick?

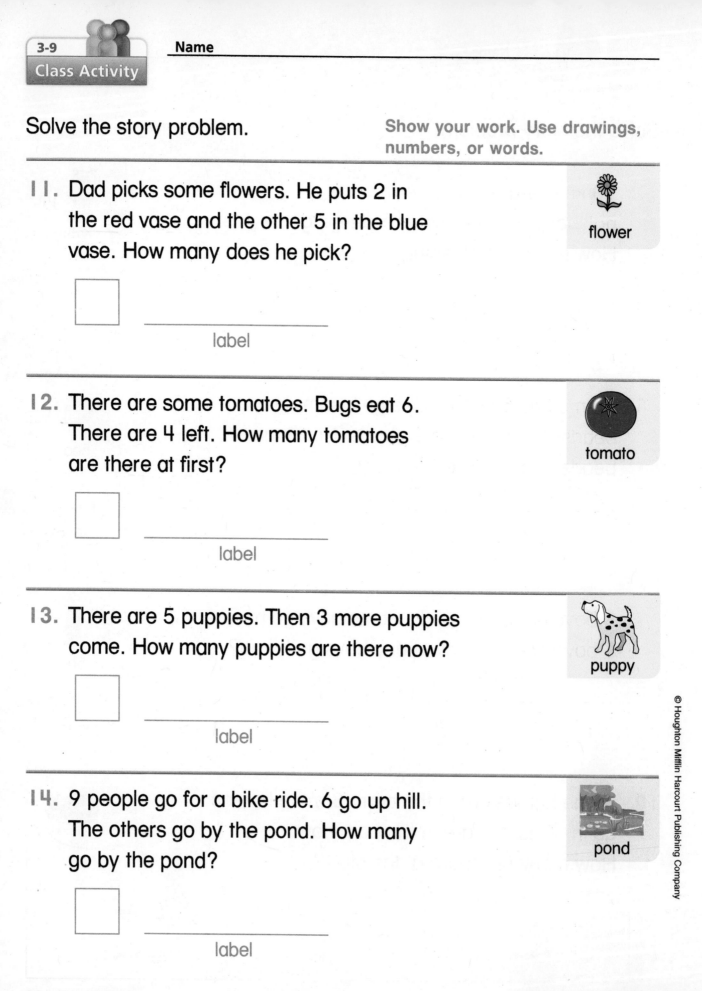

flower

☐ _____
   label

12. There are some tomatoes. Bugs eat 6. There are 4 left. How many tomatoes are there at first?

tomato

☐ _____
   label

13. There are 5 puppies. Then 3 more puppies come. How many puppies are there now?

puppy

☐ _____
   label

14. 9 people go for a bike ride. 6 go up hill. The others go by the pond. How many go by the pond?

pond

☐ _____
   label

Solve.

1. Sam scores 4 points. Julio scores 3 points. How many points do they score in all?

2. Sam scores 4 points. Julio also scores some points. In all they score 7 points. How many points does Julio score?

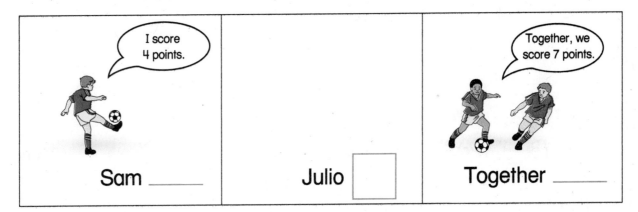

3. Sam scores some points. Then Julio scores 3 points. In all they score 7 points. How many points does Sam score?

Name _____

Solve the story problem.

Show your work. Use drawings, numbers, or words.

4. 8 frogs are in the pond. Some hop away.
2 are left. How many frogs hop away?

pond

☐ _____
        label

5. Ivan has some balls.
He gives 4 to friends.
He has 3 left. How many
did he have before?

ball

☐ _____
        label

6. There are 7 flowers. Sam picks 2.
How many flowers are left?

flower

☐ _____
        label

PATH to FLUENCY Subtract.

1. $2 - 2 = $ ☐   **2.** $4 - 2 = $ ☐   **3.** $4 - 4 = $ ☐

4. $8 - 4 = $ ☐   **5.** $5 - 5 = $ ☐   **6.** $10 - 5 = $ ☐

Solve Mixed Problems

Number Quilt 3: Any Unknown

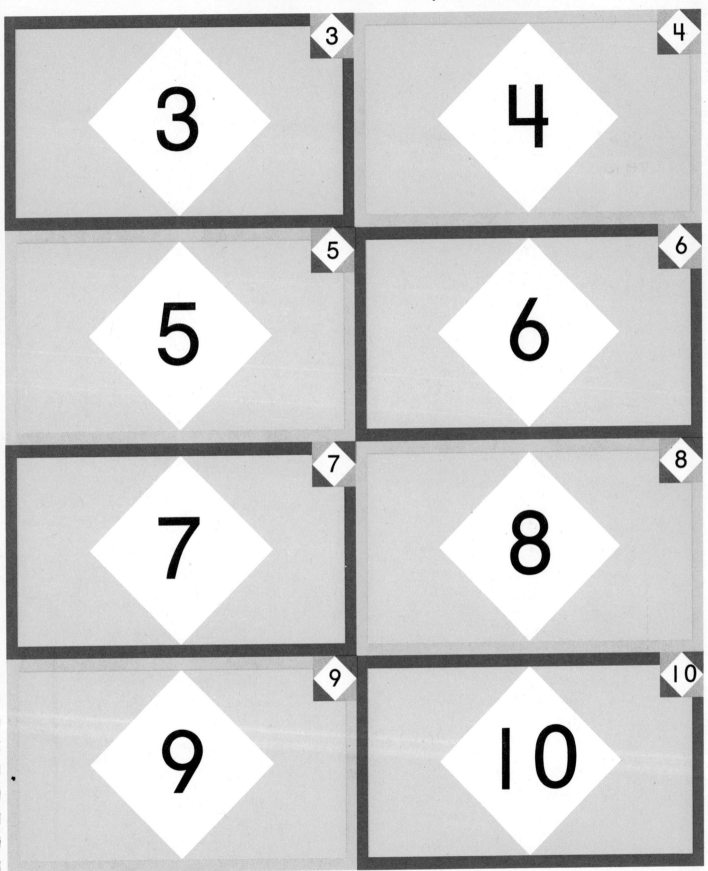

Use with any of the Count-On Cards.

Math and Sports

Write the equation to solve.

1. There are 7 balls in the box.
Jabar puts some more balls
in the box. Now there are 10 balls
in the box. How many balls
does Jabar put in the box?

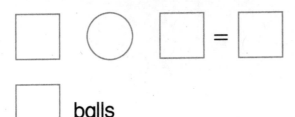

□ balls

2. There were 8 baseballs in the
bucket. Leslie takes some
baseballs from the bucket.
Now there are 6 baseballs in
the bucket. How many baseballs
does Leslie take?

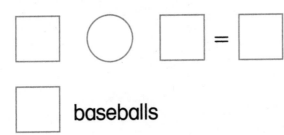

□ baseballs

© Houghton Mifflin Harcourt Publishing Company

3. Use the picture to write a story problem.
Write and solve the equation.

_____

- -

_____

- -

_____

- -

_____

- -

_____

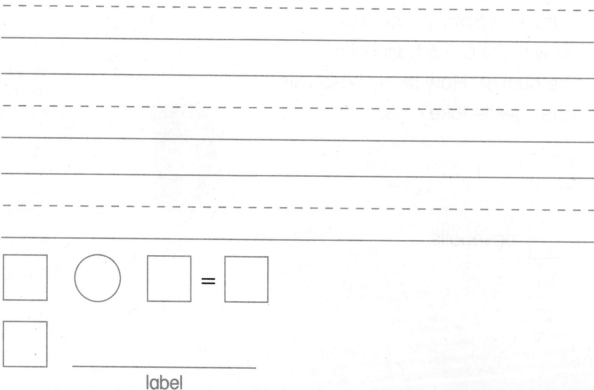

□ ◯ □ = □

□ _____
    label

Find the unknown partner or total. Watch the signs.

1. $7 + 3 = \boxed{}$

2. $5 + 4 = \boxed{}$

3. $4 + \boxed{} = 10$

4. $5 + \boxed{} = 8$

5. $7 - 3 = \boxed{}$

6. $10 - 2 = \boxed{}$

7. $8 - \boxed{} = 2$

8. $10 - \boxed{} = 7$

Solve the story problem.

Show your work. Use drawings, numbers, or words.

9. Dinah has 7 orange seashells
and 3 white seashells.
How many seashells does
she have in all?

seashell

$\boxed{}$ _____
          label

10. There are 5 bees in the garden.
Then 4 more bees come.
How many bees are there in all?

garden

$\boxed{}$ _____
          label

Solve the story problem.

Show your work. Use drawings, numbers, or words.

11. Al puts 3 pens on the table. He puts the rest on the shelf. Altogether there are 9 pens. How many are on the shelf?

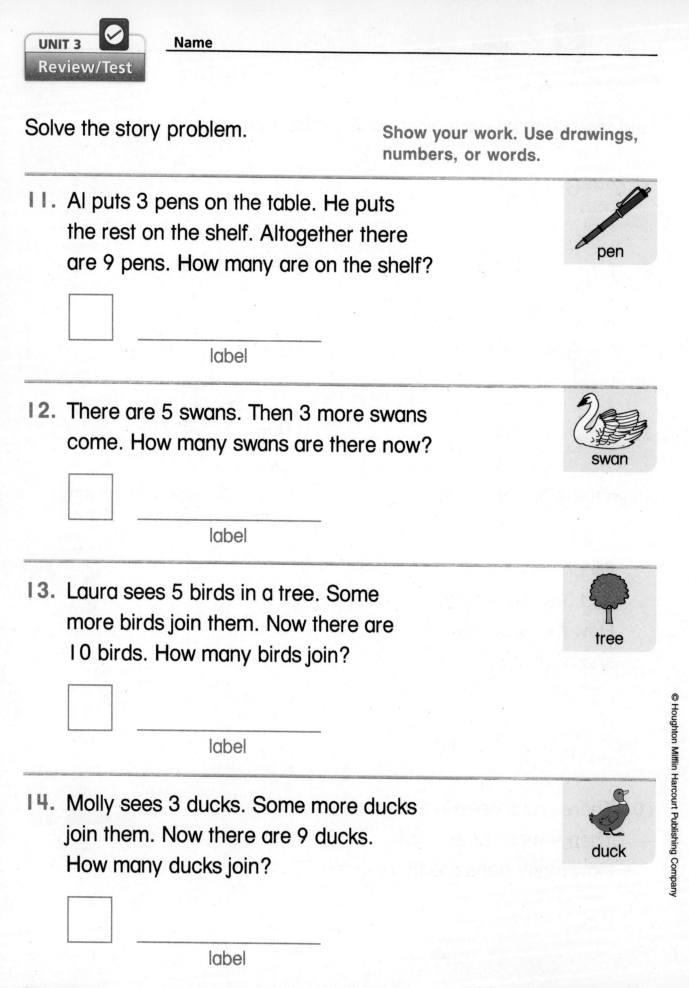

pen

☐ _____
label

12. There are 5 swans. Then 3 more swans come. How many swans are there now?

swan

☐ _____
label

13. Laura sees 5 birds in a tree. Some more birds join them. Now there are 10 birds. How many birds join?

tree

☐ _____
label

14. Molly sees 3 ducks. Some more ducks join them. Now there are 9 ducks. How many ducks join?

duck

☐ _____
label

Solve the story problem.

Show your work. Use drawings, numbers, or words.

---

15. Sam has 9 kittens. He gives 6 away. How many are left?

kitten

☐   _____

label

---

16. Rosa picks 9 carrots. She gives some away. Now she has 5. How many does she give away?

carrot

☐   _____

label

---

17. There are 10 rabbits in a field. Then 3 run away. How many rabbits are left?

rabbit

☐   _____

label

---

18. Ed has 7 flowers in a vase. Then he gives some away. Now he has 4. How many flowers does he give away?

vase

☐   _____

label

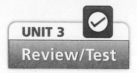
Solve the story problem.

Show your work. Use drawings, numbers, or words.

19. Ed wants to put 9 buttons in a box. He wants to have green buttons and red buttons. How many of each color can he have? Show three answers.

button

☐ green buttons and ☐ red buttons

or ☐ green buttons and ☐ red buttons

or ☐ green buttons and ☐ red buttons

20. **Extended Response.** Read the story problem. Write a subtraction and an addition equation for the story. Draw a Math Mountain to match.

8 dogs are running on the beach.
5 dogs go home.
How many dogs are on the beach now?

Dear Family:

Your child is learning about place value and numbers to 100. In this program, children begin by counting tens: 10, 20, 30, 40, and so on. They use a 10 × 10 Grid to help them "see" the relationship between the tens digit in a decade number and the number of tens it has.

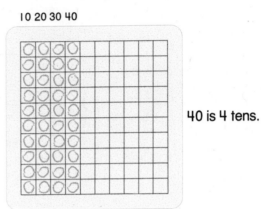

40 is 4 tens.

Soon, children will link 2-digit numbers to tens and extra ones. They will learn that a 2-digit number, such as 46, is made up of tens and ones, such as 40 and 6. Next, children will use what they know about adding 1-digit numbers to add 2-digit numbers.

$$3 + 4 = 7, \text{ so } 30 + 40 = 70.$$

Finally, they will learn to regroup and count on to find a total. For example:

$$19 + 5 = \boxed{24}$$

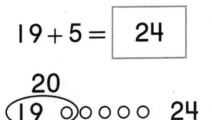

Right now, your child may enjoy counting by tens for you. He or she may also enjoy using household items to make groups of ten and extra ones, and then telling you the total number.

Sincerely,
Your child's teacher

COMMON CORE Unit 4 includes the Common Core Standards for Mathematical Content for Operations and Algebraic Thinking 1.OA.1, 1.OA.5, 1.OA.6; Number and Operations in Base Ten, 1.NBT.1, 1.NBT.2, 1.NBT.2a, 1.NBT.2b, 1.NBT.2c, 1.NBT.3, 1.NBT.4 and all Mathematical Practices.

Estimada familia:

Su niño está aprendiendo sobre valor posicional y los números hasta 100. En este programa, los niños empiezan contando decenas: 10, 20, 30, 40, etc. Usan una cuadrícula de 10 por 10 como ayuda para "ver" la relación entre el dígito de las decenas en el número que termina en cero y el número de decenas que tiene.

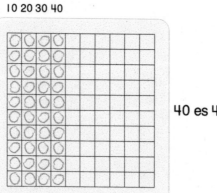

10 20 30 40

40 es 4 decenas.

En poco tiempo, los niños harán la conexión entre números de 2 dígitos y decenas más otras unidades. Aprenderán que un número de 2 dígitos, tal como 46, consta de decenas y unidades, como 40 y 6. Luego, los niños usarán lo que saben de la suma de números de 1 dígito para sumar números de 2 dígitos.

$$3 + 4 = 7, \text{ por lo tanto } 30 + 40 = 70.$$

Finalmente, aprenderán a reagrupar y contar hacia adelante para hallar el total. Por ejemplo:

$$19 + 5 = \boxed{24}$$

20
(19) ○○○○○ 24

Por lo pronto, tal vez a su niño le guste contar en decenas para Ud. También puede gustarle usar objetos del hogar para formar grupos de diez más otras unidades y luego decir el número total.

Atentamente,
El maestro de su niño

COMMON CORE La Unidad 4 incluye los Common Core Standards for Mathematical Content for Operations and Algebraic Thinking 1.OA.1, 1.OA.5, 1.OA.6; Number and Operations in Base Ten, 1.NBT.1, 1.NBT.2, 1.NBT.2a, 1.NBT.2b, 1.NBT.2c, 1.NBT.3, 1.NBT.4 and all Mathematical Practices.

VOCABULARY
tens

How many circles? Count by **tens**.

1.

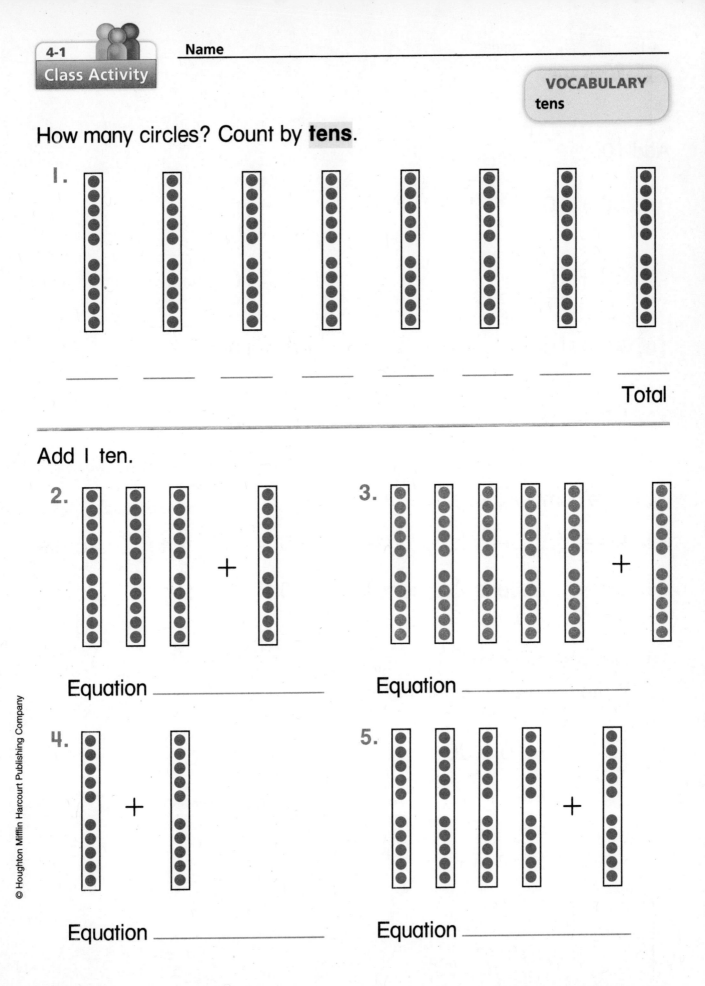

___ ___ ___ ___ ___ ___ ___ ___

Total

Add 1 ten.

2.

+

Equation _____

3.

+

Equation _____

4.

+

Equation _____

5.

+

Equation _____

© Houghton Mifflin Harcourt Publishing Company

Add 10.

6. 50 + 10 = ⬜

7. 10 + 10 = ⬜

8. 30 + 10 = ⬜

9. 80 + 10 = ⬜

10. 70 + 10 = ⬜

11. 60 + 10 = ⬜

12. 40 + 10 = ⬜

13. 90 + 10 = ⬜

Write the numbers.

14. 20 = ____ tens ____ ones

15. 80 = ____ tens ____ ones

16. 50 = ____ tens ____ ones

17. 10 = ____ ten ____ ones

18. Draw tens to solve.
    Write the unknown number.

⬜ + 10 = 30

Introduction to Tens Groupings

Dear Family:

To help children "see" the tens and ones in 2-digit numbers, the *Math Expressions* program uses special drawings of 10-sticks to show tens, and circles to show ones. These images help children learn place value. Below are the numbers 27 and 52 shown with 10-sticks and circles:

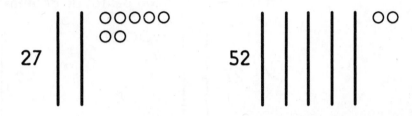

10-sticks and circles will also be used later to help children solve addition problems that require regrouping (sometimes called "carrying"). When there are enough circles to make a new ten, they are circled and then added like a 10-stick. The problem below shows 38 + 5:

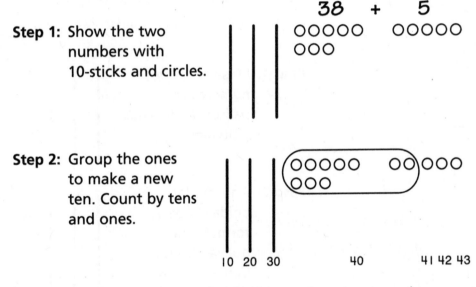

Step 1: Show the two numbers with 10-sticks and circles.

Step 2: Group the ones to make a new ten. Count by tens and ones.

Right now, your child is just beginning to show teen numbers with 10-sticks and circles. Soon your child will be able to draw 10-sticks and circles for any 2-digit number.

Sincerely,
Your child's teacher

COMMON CORE Unit 4 includes the Common Core Standards for Mathematical Content for Operations and Algebraic Thinking 1.OA.1, 1.OA.5, 1.OA.6; Number and Operations in Base Ten, 1.NBT.1, 1.NBT.2, 1.NBT.2a, 1.NBT.2b, 1.NBT.2c, 1.NBT.3, 1.NBT.4 and all Mathematical Practices.

Estimada familia:

Para ayudar a los niños a "ver" las decenas y las unidades en los números de 2 dígitos, el programa *Math Expressions* usa dibujos especiales de palitos de decenas para mostrar las decenas, y círculos para mostrar las unidades. Estas imágenes ayudan a los niños a aprender el valor posicional. Abajo se muestran los números 27 y 52 con palitos de decenas y círculos:

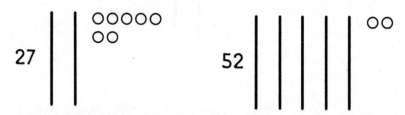

Más adelante, los palitos de decenas y los círculos también se usarán para ayudar a los niños a resolver problemas de suma que requieren reagrupar (que a veces se llama "llevar"). Cuando hay suficientes círculos para formar una nueva decena, se encierran en un círculo y se suman como si fueran un palito de decena. El siguiente problema muestra 38 + 5:

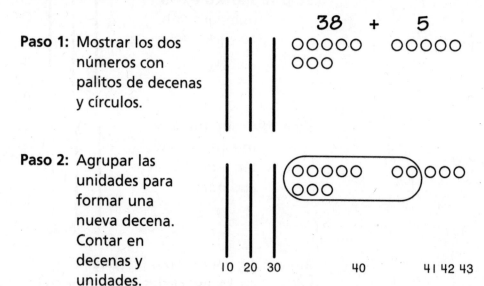

Paso 1: Mostrar los dos números con palitos de decenas y círculos.

Paso 2: Agrupar las unidades para formar una nueva decena. Contar en decenas y unidades.

Su niño está comenzando a mostrar los números de 11 a 19 con palitos de decenas y círculos. Pronto, podrá dibujar palitos de decenas y círculos para cualquier número de 2 dígitos.

Atentamente,
El maestro de su niño

COMMON CORE

La Unidad 4 incluye los Common Core Standards for Mathematical Content for Operations and Algebraic Thinking 1.OA.1, 1.OA.5, 1.OA.6; Number and Operations in Base Ten, 1.NBT.1, 1.NBT.2, 1.NBT.2a, 1.NBT.2b, 1.NBT.2c, 1.NBT.3, 1.NBT.4 and all Mathematical Practices.

Represent and Compare Teen Numbers

1. Look at what Puzzled Penguin wrote.

$$7 + 8 = 10 + \boxed{3}$$

$$7 + 8 = \boxed{13}$$

Am I correct?

2. Help Puzzled Penguin.

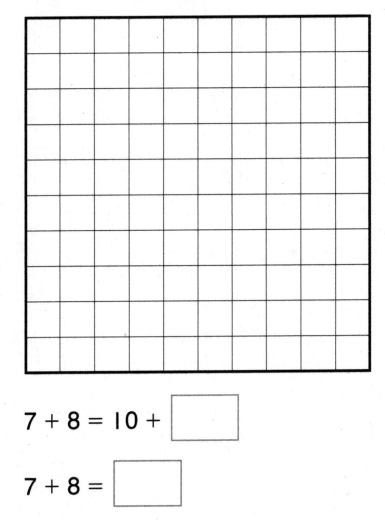

$$7 + 8 = 10 + \boxed{}$$

$$7 + 8 = \boxed{}$$

Find the total. Then **make a ten**.

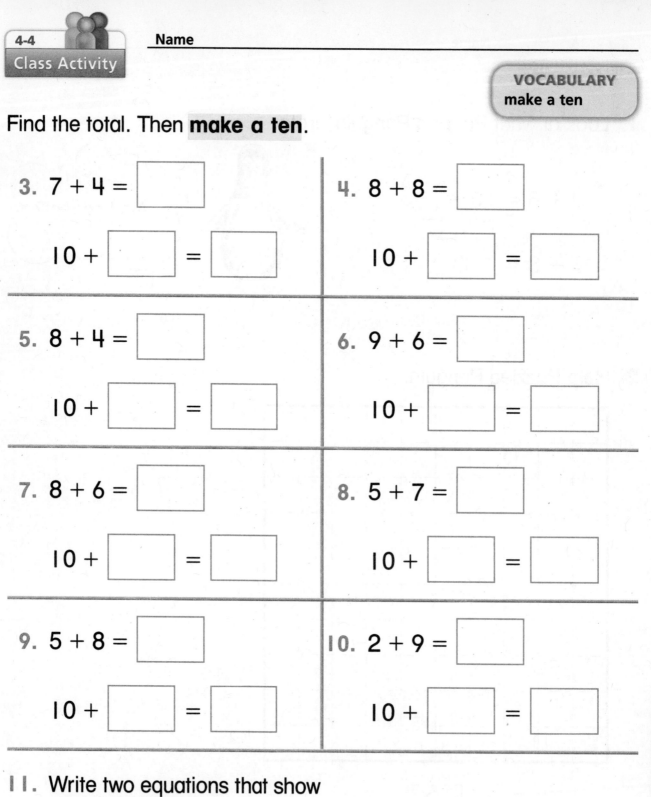

3. $7 + 4 =$ ☐

$10 +$ ☐ $=$ ☐

4. $8 + 8 =$ ☐

$10 +$ ☐ $=$ ☐

5. $8 + 4 =$ ☐

$10 +$ ☐ $=$ ☐

6. $9 + 6 =$ ☐

$10 +$ ☐ $=$ ☐

7. $8 + 6 =$ ☐

$10 +$ ☐ $=$ ☐

8. $5 + 7 =$ ☐

$10 +$ ☐ $=$ ☐

9. $5 + 8 =$ ☐

$10 +$ ☐ $=$ ☐

10. $2 + 9 =$ ☐

$10 +$ ☐ $=$ ☐

11. Write two equations that show
different partners for 13.
Use 10 in one equation.

_____

_____

Visualize Teen Addition

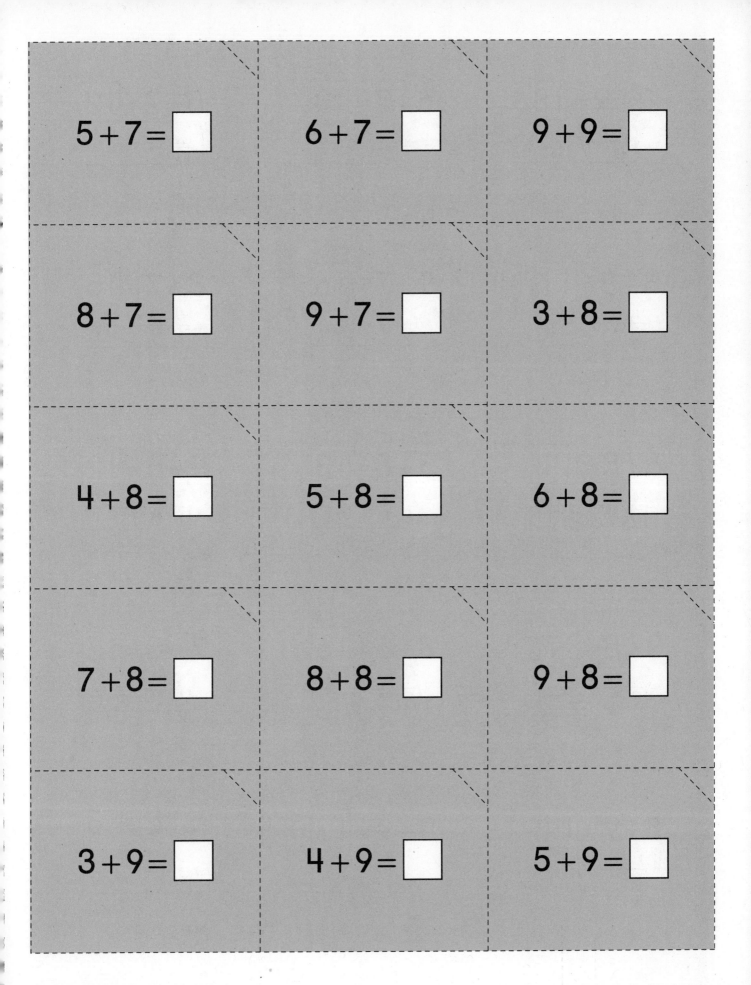

5 + 7 = ☐   6 + 7 = ☐   9 + 9 = ☐

8 + 7 = ☐   9 + 7 = ☐   3 + 8 = ☐

4 + 8 = ☐   5 + 8 = ☐   6 + 8 = ☐

7 + 8 = ☐   8 + 8 = ☐   9 + 8 = ☐

3 + 9 = ☐   4 + 9 = ☐   5 + 9 = ☐

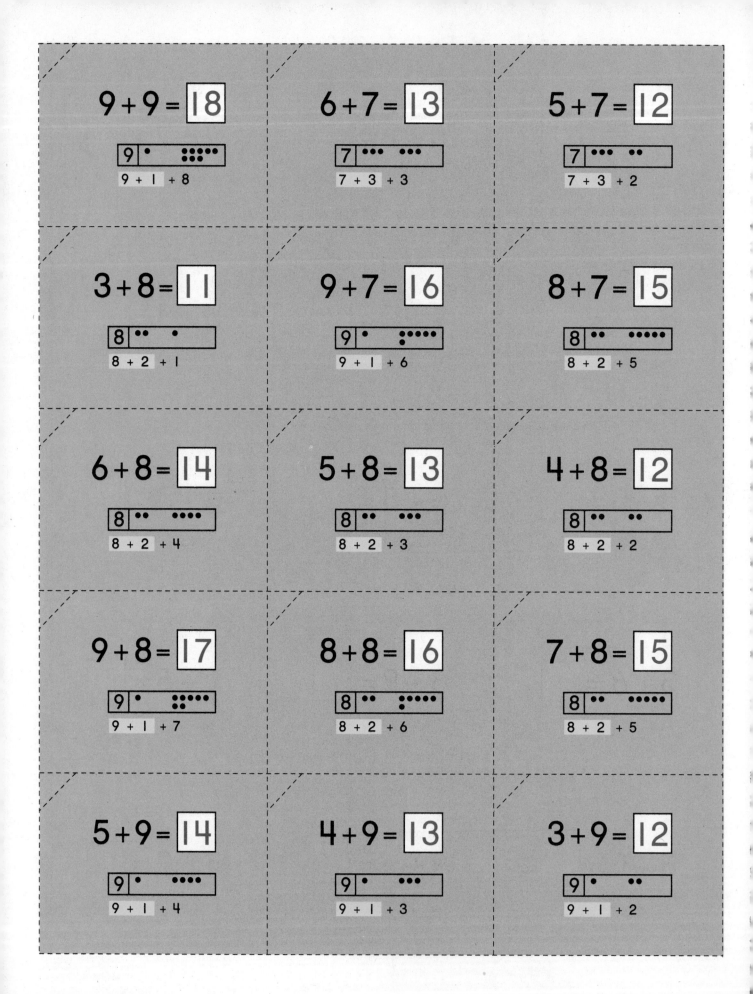

9 + 9 = 18

9 + 1 + 8

6 + 7 = 13

7 + 3 + 3

5 + 7 = 12

7 + 3 + 2

3 + 8 = 11

8 + 2 + 1

9 + 7 = 16

9 + 1 + 6

8 + 7 = 15

8 + 2 + 5

6 + 8 = 14

8 + 2 + 4

5 + 8 = 13

8 + 2 + 3

4 + 8 = 12

8 + 2 + 2

9 + 8 = 17

9 + 1 + 7

8 + 8 = 16

8 + 2 + 6

7 + 8 = 15

8 + 2 + 5

5 + 9 = 14

9 + 1 + 4

4 + 9 = 13

9 + 1 + 3

3 + 9 = 12

9 + 1 + 2

Green Make-a-Ten Cards

6 + 9 = ☐   7 + 9 = ☐   7 + 4 = ☐

8 + 4 = ☐   9 + 4 = ☐   6 + 5 = ☐

7 + 5 = ☐   8 + 5 = ☐   9 + 5 = ☐

5 + 6 = ☐   8 + 9 = ☐   7 + 6 = ☐

8 + 6 = ☐   9 + 6 = ☐   4 + 7 = ☐

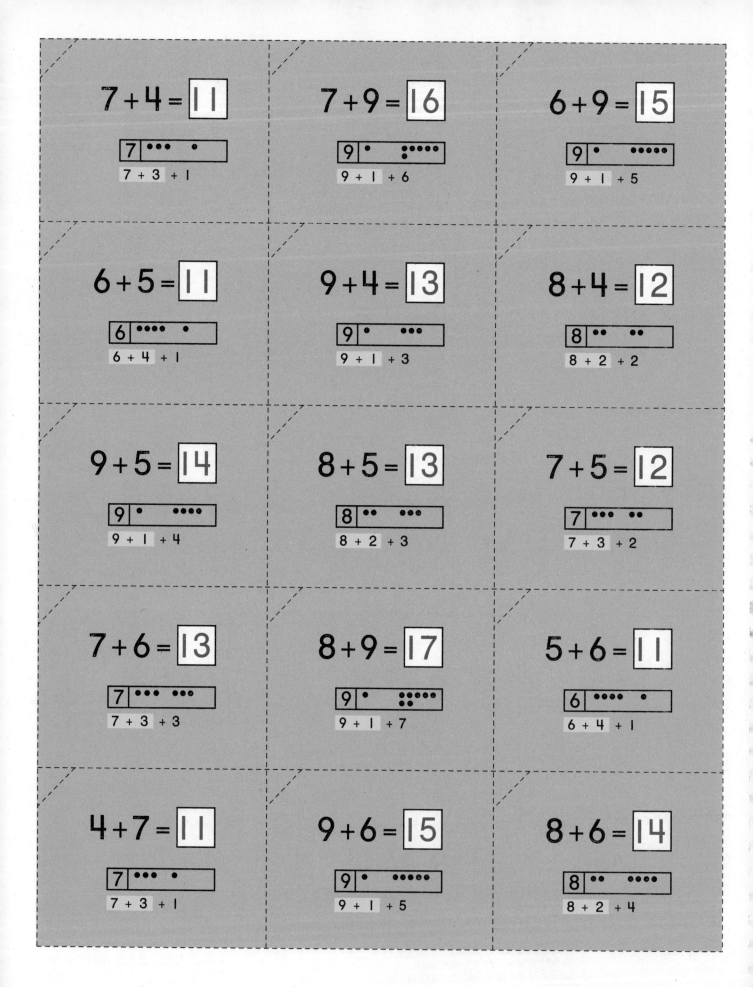

Green Make-a-Ten Cards

Find the teen total.

1. 5 + 9 = ☐

2. 7 + 5 = ☐

3. 7 + 4 = ☐

4. 9 + 6 = ☐

5. 9 + 8 = ☐

6. 9 + 9 = ☐

7. 3 + 9 = ☐

8. 7 + 8 = ☐

9. 9 + 4 = ☐

10. 6 + 5 = ☐

11. 8 + 8 = ☐

12. 8 + 4 = ☐

13. 7 + 6 = ☐

14. 9 + 7 = ☐

15. Write an equation with a teen total.
Draw or explain how making a ten
can help you solve your equation.

☐

Find the total.

16. 10 + 9 = ☐

17. 9 + 10 = ☐

18. 6 + 4 = ☐

19. 10 + 3 = ☐

20. 10 + 8 = ☐

21. 3 + 10 = ☐

22. 1 + 9 = ☐

23. 10 + 10 = ☐

24. Draw or write to explain how
     you solved Exercise 23.

Use **doubles** to find the total.

1. $5 + 5 = $ ☐   2. $6 + 6 = $ ☐   3. $7 + 7 = $ ☐

4. $8 + 8 = $ ☐   5. $9 + 9 = $ ☐   6. $10 + 10 = $ ☐

Use **doubles plus 1** or **doubles minus 1** to find the total.

7. $4 + 4 = 8$
$4 + 5 = 8 + \text{\_\_\_} = \text{\_\_\_}$

8. $8 + 8 = 16$
$8 + 7 = 16 - \text{\_\_\_} = \text{\_\_\_}$

9. $5 + 6 = $ ☐   10. $9 + 8 = $ ☐   11. $6 + 7 = $ ☐

Use **doubles plus 2** or **doubles minus 2** to find the total.

12. $4 + 4 = 8$
$4 + 6 = 8 + \text{\_\_\_} = \text{\_\_\_}$

13. $8 + 8 = 16$
$8 + 6 = 16 - \text{\_\_\_} = \text{\_\_\_}$

14. $7 + 5 = $ ☐   15. $7 + 9 = $ ☐   16. $6 + 8 = $ ☐

Use a double to find the total.

17.   8
    + 7

18. 10
    + 8

19.   5
    + 7

20.   6
    + 5

21.   8
    + 9

22.   7
    + 8

23.   7
    + 5

24.   7
    + 6

25. Write the double you used to solve Exercise 23.

_____

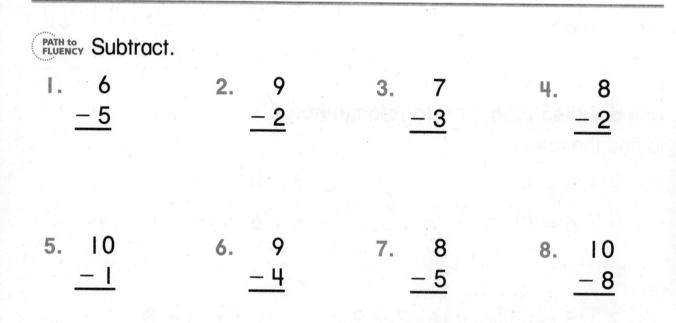

PATH to FLUENCY **Subtract.**

1.   6
   − 5

2.   9
   − 2

3.   7
   − 3

4.   8
   − 2

5. 10
   − 1

6.   9
   − 4

7.   8
   − 5

8. 10
   − 8

Investigate Doubles

1 one	11 eleven	10 ten
2 two	12 twelve	20 twenty
3 three	13 thirteen	30 thirty
4 four	14 fourteen	40 forty
5 five	15 fifteen	50 fifty
6 six	16 sixteen	60 sixty
7 seven	17 seventeen	70 seventy
8 eight	18 eighteen	80 eighty
9 nine	19 nineteen	90 ninety
10 ten	20 twenty	

Write the number.

1. five _____   fifteen _____   fifty _____

2. three _____   thirteen _____   thirty _____

3. two _____   twelve _____   twenty _____

4. sixty _____   sixteen _____   six _____

5. eighteen _____   eighty _____   eight _____

Write the number word.

6. 4 _____   14 _____   40 _____

7. 9 _____   19 _____   90 _____

8. 2 _____   12 _____   20 _____

9. 70 _____   17 _____   7 _____

10. 1 _____   10 _____   11 _____

1 one	11 eleven	10 ten
2 two	12 twelve	20 twenty
3 three	13 thirteen	30 thirty
4 four	14 fourteen	40 forty
5 five	15 fifteen	50 fifty
6 six	16 sixteen	60 sixty
7 seven	17 seventeen	70 seventy
8 eight	18 eighteen	80 eighty
9 nine	19 nineteen	90 ninety

Write the number word.

11. | ○○ _____

12. || _____

13. | ○○○ _____

14. ○○○ _____

15. ||||| _____

16. | ○○○○○ _____

17. Write the numbers 1–20.

									20

18. Write the decade numbers 10–90.

10	20							

Integrate Tens and Ones

Each box has 10 muffins. How many muffins are there?

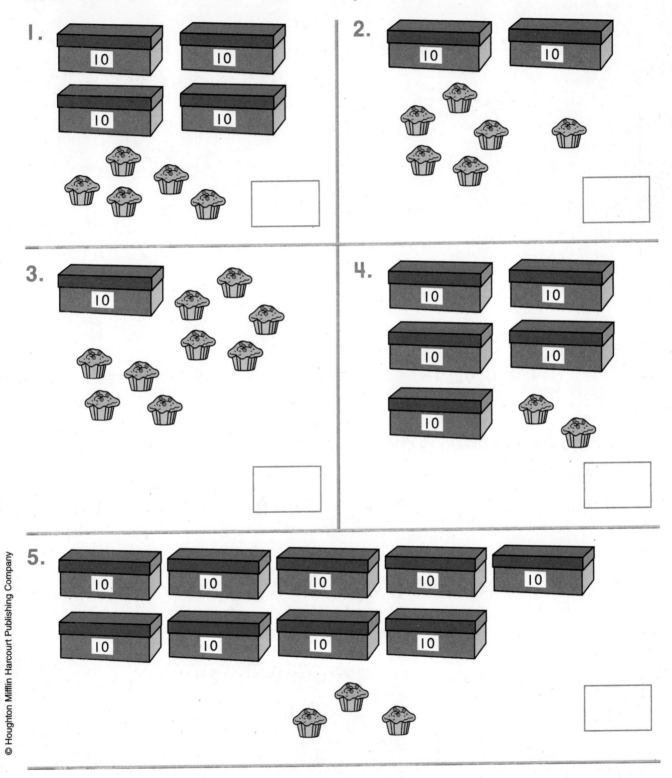

6. **Discuss** How are 23 and 32 the same? How are they different?

PATH to FLUENCY **Add.**

1. $3 + 3 =$ ☐   2. $4 + 5 =$ ☐   3. $1 + 5 =$ ☐

4. $3 + 7 =$ ☐   5. $8 + 0 =$ ☐   6. $2 + 5 =$ ☐

7. $4 + 2 =$ ☐   8. $4 + 4 =$ ☐   9. $3 + 6 =$ ☐

10. ☐ $= 5 + 2$ 11. ☐ $= 7 + 1$ 12. ☐ $= 5 + 5$

13. ☐ $= 1 + 6$ 14. ☐ $= 7 + 3$ 15. ☐ $= 5 + 3$

PATH to FLUENCY **Find the unknown number.**

16. $2 +$ ☐ $= 9$ 17. $6 +$ ☐ $= 10$ 18. $4 +$ ☐ $= 7$

19. $8 +$ ☐ $= 10$ 20. $3 +$ ☐ $= 8$ 21. $1 +$ ☐ $= 10$

22. ☐ $+ 3 = 9$ 23. ☐ $+ 6 = 8$ 24. ☐ $+ 8 = 9$

25. ☐ $+ 6 = 6$ 26. ☐ $+ 4 = 7$ 27. ☐ $+ 2 = 9$

Add with Groups of Ten

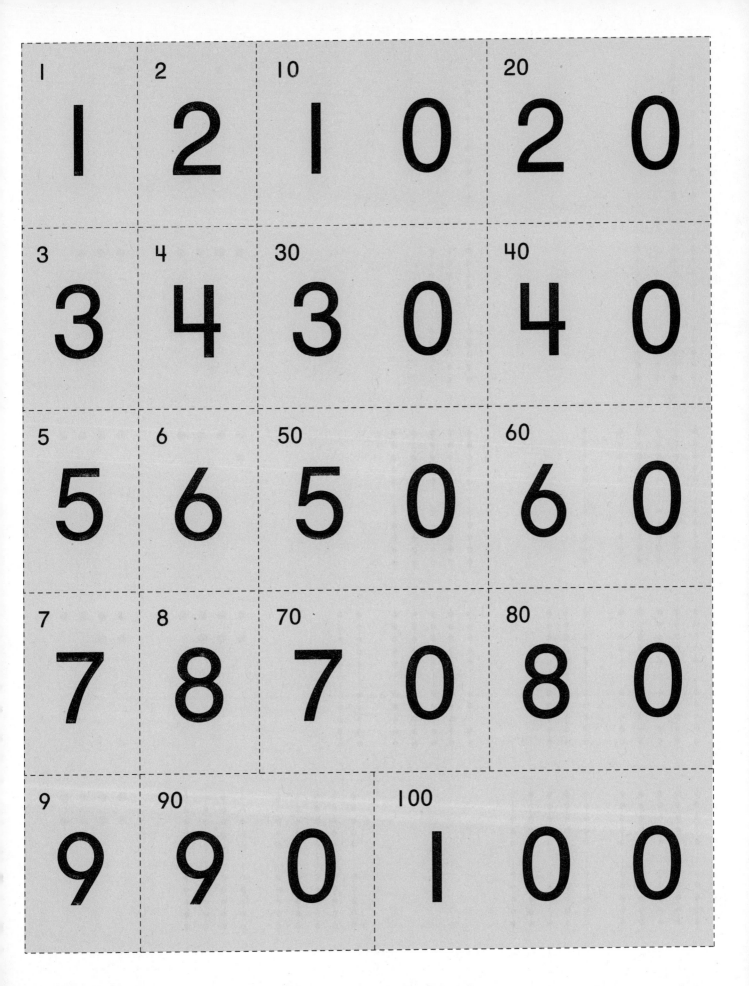

Secret Code Cards

Compare the numbers. Write >, <, or =.

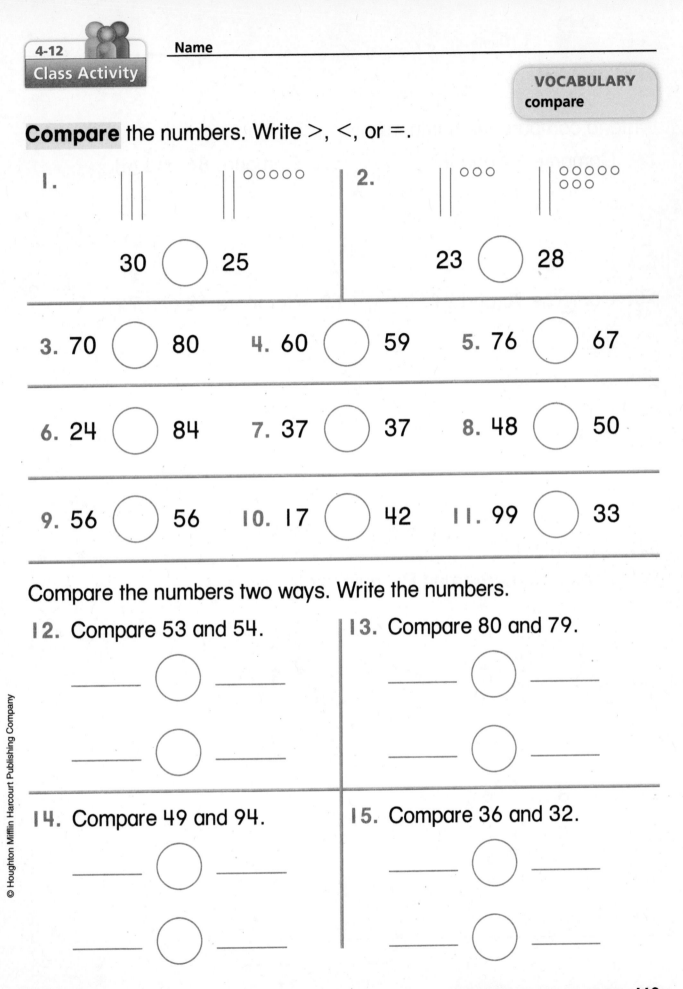

1. ||| ○○○○○
   30 ◯ 25

2. || ○○○ || ○○○○○ ○○○
   23 ◯ 28

3. 70 ◯ 80   4. 60 ◯ 59   5. 76 ◯ 67

6. 24 ◯ 84   7. 37 ◯ 37   8. 48 ◯ 50

9. 56 ◯ 56   10. 17 ◯ 42   11. 99 ◯ 33

Compare the numbers two ways. Write the numbers.

12. Compare 53 and 54.

___ ◯ ___

___ ◯ ___

13. Compare 80 and 79.

___ ◯ ___

___ ◯ ___

14. Compare 49 and 94.

___ ◯ ___

___ ◯ ___

15. Compare 36 and 32.

___ ◯ ___

___ ◯ ___

Write to compare the numbers.

16. Compare 39 and 40.

_____ ◯ _____

17. Compare 86 and 68.

_____ ◯ _____

18. Compare 95 and 91.

_____ ◯ _____

19. Compare 72 and 72.

_____ ◯ _____

20. Compare 20 and 10.

_____ ◯ _____

21. Compare 60 and 16.

_____ ◯ _____

22. Look at what Puzzled Penguin wrote.

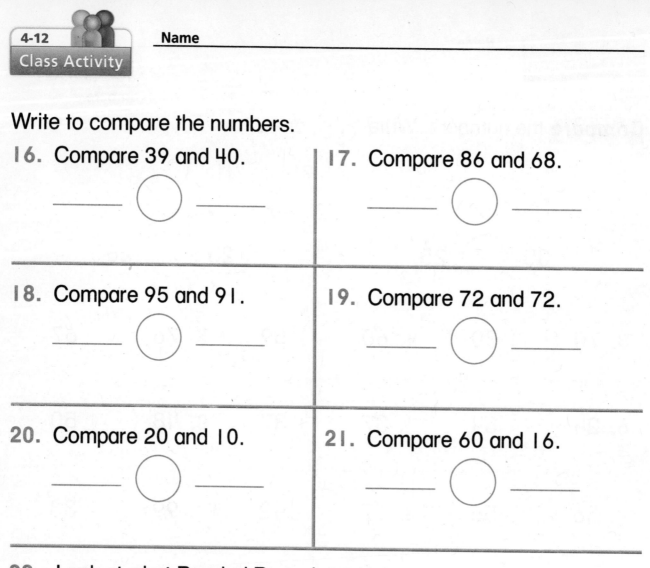

29 (>) 36

Am I correct?

23. Help Puzzled Penguin.

29 ◯ 36

Solve.

1. 3 + 6 = _____
   30 + 60 = _____
   30 + 6 = _____

2. 4 + 5 = _____
   40 + 50 = _____
   40 + 5 = _____

3. 2 + 4 = _____
   20 + 40 = _____
   20 + 4 = _____

4. 5 + 2 = _____
   50 + 20 = _____
   50 + 2 = _____

5. 7 + 2 = _____
   70 + 20 = _____
   70 + 2 = _____

6. 4 + 1 = _____
   40 + 10 = _____
   40 + 1 = _____

7. 3 + 2 = _____
   30 + 20 = _____
   30 + 2 = _____

8. 1 + 8 = _____
   10 + 80 = _____
   10 + 8 = _____

Complete the set of equations to follow the
same rules as each set above. Then solve.

9. 3 + 5 = _____
   30 + _____ = _____
   30 + _____ = _____

10. 4 + 3 = _____
    40 + _____ = _____
    40 + _____ = _____

Name _____

Find the unknown numbers to complete
the set of equations.

11. $2 + $ _____ $= 5$

  $20 + 30 = $ _____

  $20 + $ _____ $= 23$

12. $4 + $ _____ $= 8$

  _____ $+ 40 = 80$

  $40 + 4 = $ _____

13. _____ $+ 2 = 6$

  $40 + $ _____ $= 60$

  _____ $+ 2 = 42$

14. _____ $+ 7 = 8$

  $10 + $ _____ $= 80$

  $10 + 7 = $ _____

15. Look at what Puzzled Penguin wrote.

$50 + 4 = \boxed{90}$

Am I correct?

16. Help Puzzled Penguin.

  $50 + 4 = \boxed{}$

Mixed Addition with Tens and Ones

Here is a riddle.

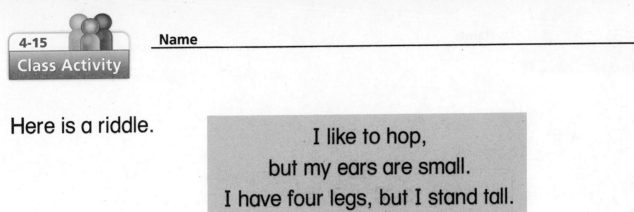

I like to hop,
but my ears are small.
I have four legs, but I stand tall.
I have a pocket,
but I cannot buy.
Guess my name. Who am I?

Find the total. Use any method.

1. $46 + 5 =$ ☐ O

2. $40 + 2 =$ ☐ O

3. $12 + 7 =$ ☐ K

4. $29 + 5 =$ ☐ R

5. $64 + 6 =$ ☐ A

6. $20 + 9 =$ ☐ A

7. $27 + 5 =$ ☐ G

8. $89 + 2 =$ ☐ N

Who am I? Write the letter for each total.

___ ___ ___ ___ ___ ___ ___ ___
19   70   91   32   29   34   42   51

PATH to FLUENCY Add.

1. $4 + 5 =$ ☐   2. $0 + 7 =$ ☐   3. $7 + 3 =$ ☐

4. $1 + 6 =$ ☐   5. $6 + 2 =$ ☐   6. $4 + 2 =$ ☐

7. $5 + 5 =$ ☐   8. $9 + 1 =$ ☐   9. $2 + 5 =$ ☐

10. ☐ $= 7 + 1$ 11. ☐ $= 3 + 6$ 12. ☐ $= 7 + 2$

13. ☐ $= 6 + 4$ 14. ☐ $= 2 + 4$ 15. ☐ $= 4 + 3$

PATH to FLUENCY Find the unknown number.

16. $1 +$ ☐ $= 8$ 17. $3 +$ ☐ $= 7$ 18. $5 +$ ☐ $= 8$

19. $8 +$ ☐ $= 10$ 20. $4 +$ ☐ $= 8$ 21. $9 +$ ☐ $= 9$

22. ☐ $+ 1 = 6$ 23. ☐ $+ 4 = 9$ 24. ☐ $+ 7 = 10$

25. ☐ $+ 8 = 9$ 26. ☐ $+ 5 = 8$ 27. ☐ $+ 8 = 10$

Use this sandwich sheet when you play
The Sandwich Game.

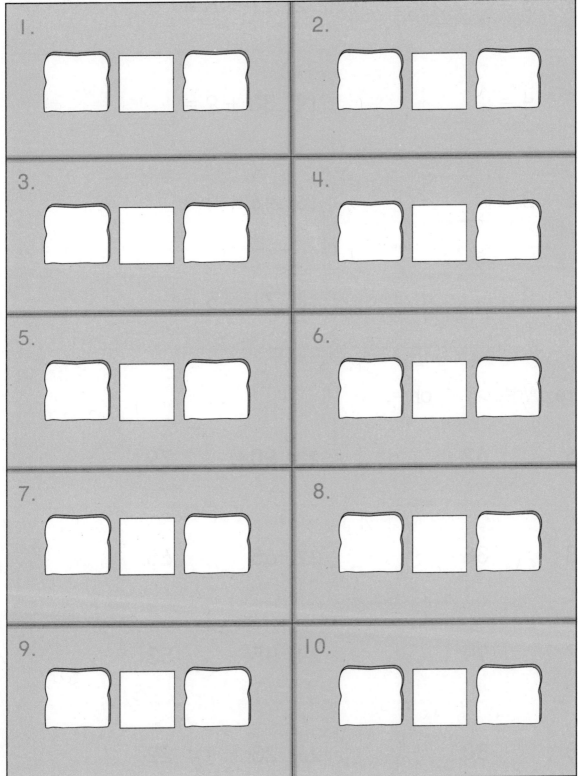

Find the total. Use any method.

11. $29 + 3 =$ ☐   12. $11 + 8 =$ ☐

13. $67 + 4 =$ ☐   14. $33 + 9 =$ ☐

15. $96 + 3 =$ ☐   16. $46 + 4 =$ ☐

17. $12 + 8 =$ ☐   18. $71 + 5 =$ ☐

Compare. Write >, <, or =.

19. 26 ◯ 62   20. 80 ◯ 79

21. 18 ◯ 38   22. 65 ◯ 65

23. 97 ◯ 94   24. 45 ◯ 53

25. 8 ◯ 80   26. 23 ◯ 22

▶ **Math and the Community Theater**

Linda and her family go to a show.

1. 10 cars can park in each row.

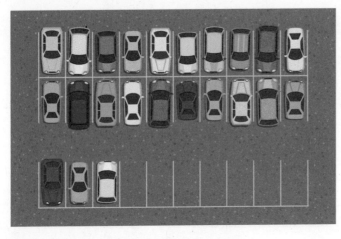

How many cars are there?

_____ tens _____ ones = _____ cars

---

2. 10 people can sit in each row.

How many people are there?

_____ tens _____ ones = _____ people

Show tickets were sold on Friday,
Saturday, and Sunday.

3. Write the number of tickets sold each day.

Friday	
	_____ tens _____ ones = _____ tickets
Saturday	
	_____ tens _____ ones = _____ tickets
Sunday	
	_____ tens _____ ones = _____ tickets

Compare the number of tickets sold.
Use >, <, or =.

4. Friday   Saturday

5. Friday   Sunday

6. Saturday   Sunday

7. Sunday   Saturday

Write the numbers.

1. 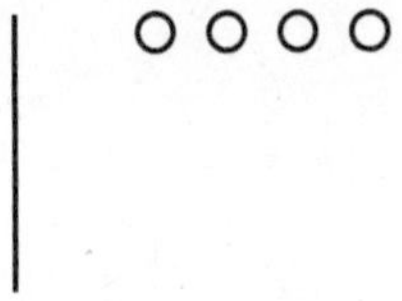 | ○ ○ ○ ○

_____ ten _____ ones = _____

2. 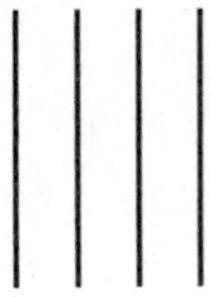 ||||

_____ tens _____ ones = _____

Draw 10-sticks and circles.

3. 26

4. 71

5. Add 1 ten.

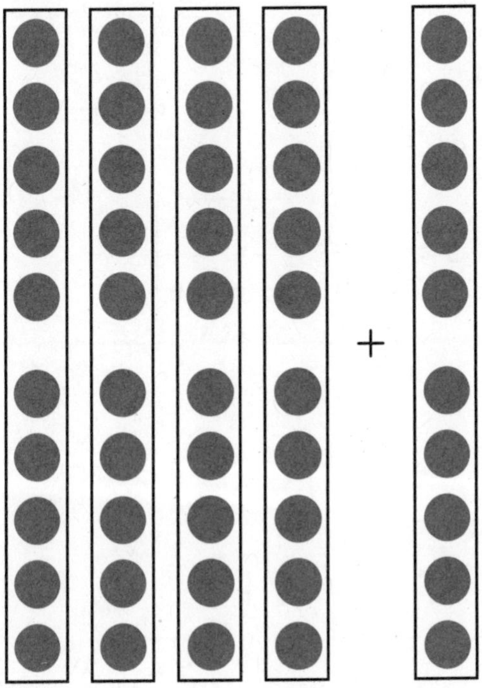

6. How many pencils?

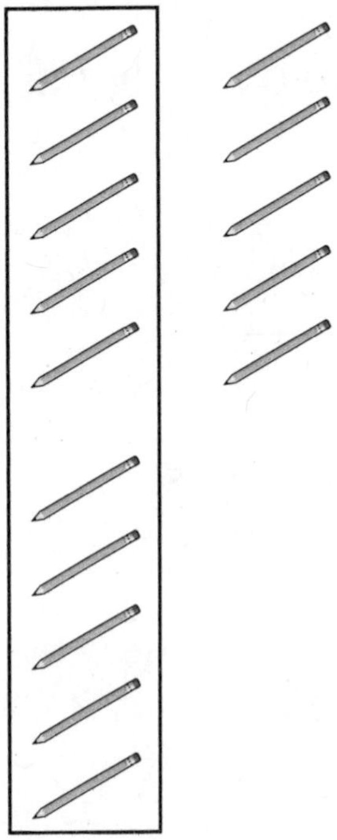

$$40 + 10 = \boxed{}$$

$$\boxed{}$$

Name _____

How many muffins are there?

7.

8.

Count on, make a ten, or use doubles.
Find the total.

9. 8 + 7 = ☐   10. 3 + 9 = ☐

Compare the numbers.
Write >, <, or =.

11. 60 ◯ 59   12. 47 ◯ 71

13. 93 ◯ 98   14. 12 ◯ 12

Solve the story problem.

15. There are 10 bagels in a bag and 9 extra bagels. How many bagels are there?

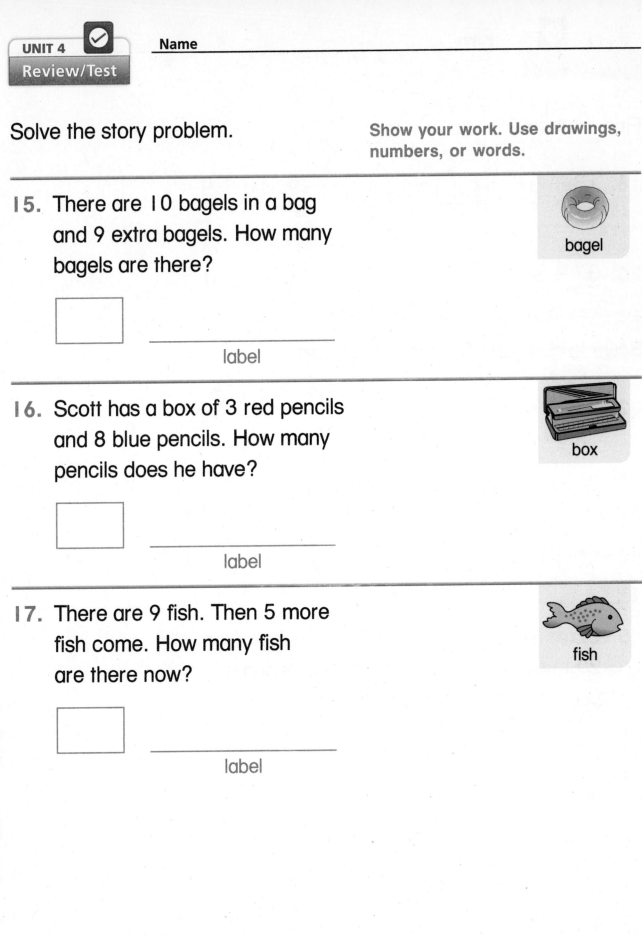

bagel

▢ _____
   label

16. Scott has a box of 3 red pencils and 8 blue pencils. How many pencils does he have?

box

▢ _____
   label

17. There are 9 fish. Then 5 more fish come. How many fish are there now?

fish

▢ _____
   label

Find the total.

18. 13 + 6 = [ ]   19. 18 + 4 = [ ]

20. 37 + 9 = [ ]   21. 79 + 1 = [ ]

Solve to complete the set of exercises.

22. 3 + 6 = [ ]

23. 30 + 60 = [ ]

24. 30 + 6 = [ ]

25. **Extended Response** Write a number from
20 to 60. Add 1 ten. Write the new number.
Draw and write to compare the numbers.

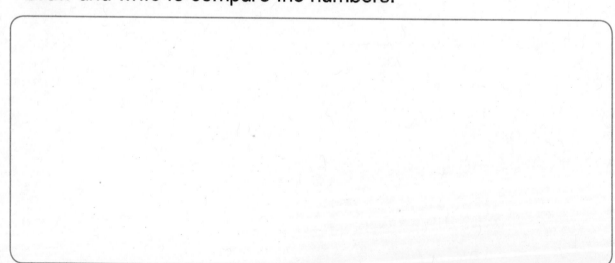

Problem Types

	Result Unknown	Change Unknown	Start Unknown
Add To	Six children are playing tag in the yard. Three more children come to play. How many children are playing in the yard now? *Situation and Solution Equation[1]:* $6 + 3 = \square$	Six children are playing tag in the yard. Some more children come to play. Now there are 9 children in the yard. How many children came to play? *Situation Equation:* $6 + \square = 9$ *Solution Equation:* $9 - 6 = \square$	Some children are playing tag in the yard. Three more children come to play. Now there are 9 children in the yard. How many children were in the yard at first? *Situation Equation:* $\square + 3 = 9$ *Solution Equation:* $9 - 3 = \square$
Take From	Jake has 10 trading cards. He gives 3 to his brother. How many trading cards does he have left? *Situation and Solution Equation:* $10 - 3 = \square$	Jake has 10 trading cards. He gives some to his brother. Now Jake has 7 trading cards left. How many cards does he give to his brother? *Situation Equation:* $10 - \square = 7$ *Solution Equation:* $10 - 7 = \square$	Jake has some trading cards. He gives 3 to his brother. Now Jake has 7 trading cards left. How many cards does he start with? *Situation Equation:* $\square - 3 = 7$ *Solution Equation:* $7 + 3 = \square$

[1]A situation equation represents the structure (action) in the problem situation. A solution equation shows the operation used to find the answer.

Problem Types (continued)

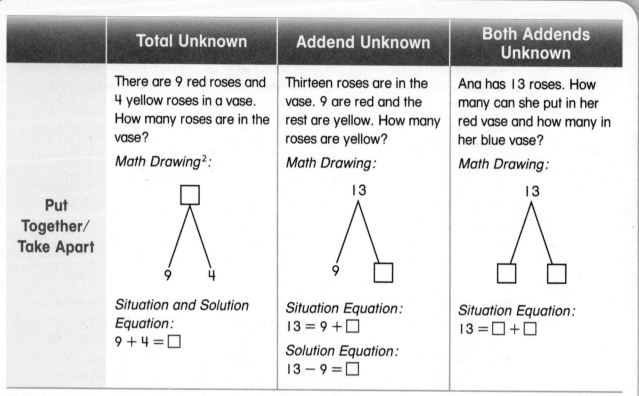

	Total Unknown	Addend Unknown	Both Addends Unknown
Put Together/ Take Apart	There are 9 red roses and 4 yellow roses in a vase. How many roses are in the vase? Math Drawing[2]: 9 4 Situation and Solution Equation: $9 + 4 = \square$	Thirteen roses are in the vase. 9 are red and the rest are yellow. How many roses are yellow? Math Drawing: 13 9 Situation Equation: $13 = 9 + \square$ Solution Equation: $13 - 9 = \square$	Ana has 13 roses. How many can she put in her red vase and how many in her blue vase? Math Drawing: 13 Situation Equation: $13 = \square + \square$

[2]These math drawings are called Math Mountains in Grades 1−3 and break-apart drawings in Grades 4 and 5.

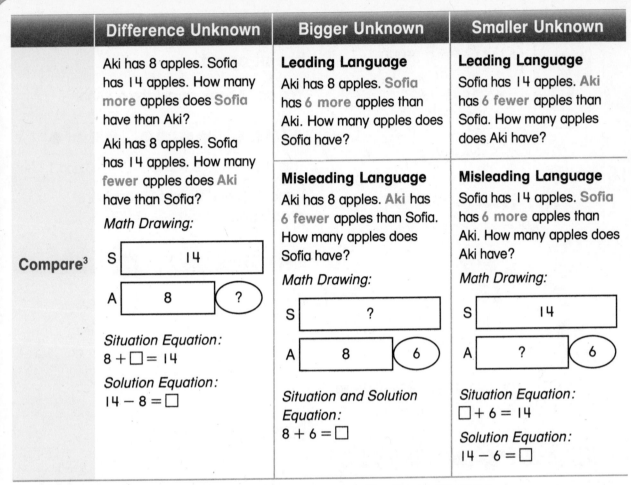

	Difference Unknown	**Bigger Unknown**	**Smaller Unknown**
Compare[3]	Aki has 8 apples. Sofia has 14 apples. How many **more** apples does **Sofia** have than Aki? Aki has 8 apples. Sofia has 14 apples. How many **fewer** apples does **Aki** have than Sofia? *Math Drawing:* S [14] A [8] (?) *Situation Equation:* $8 + \square = 14$ *Solution Equation:* $14 - 8 = \square$	**Leading Language** Aki has 8 apples. **Sofia** has 6 **more** apples than Aki. How many apples does Sofia have? **Misleading Language** Aki has 8 apples. **Aki** has 6 **fewer** apples than Sofia. How many apples does Sofia have? *Math Drawing:* S [?] A [8] (6) *Situation and Solution Equation:* $8 + 6 = \square$	**Leading Language** Sofia has 14 apples. **Aki** has 6 **fewer** apples than Sofia. How many apples does Aki have? **Misleading Language** Sofia has 14 apples. **Sofia** has 6 **more** apples than Aki. How many apples does Aki have? *Math Drawing:* S [14] A [?] (6) *Situation Equation:* $\square + 6 = 14$ *Solution Equation:* $14 - 6 = \square$

[3]A comparison sentence can always be said in two ways. One way uses *more*, and the other uses *fewer* or *less*. Misleading language suggests the wrong operation. For example, it says *Aki has 6 fewer apples than Sofia*, but you have to add 6 to Aki's 8 apples to get 14 apples.

Glossary

5-group

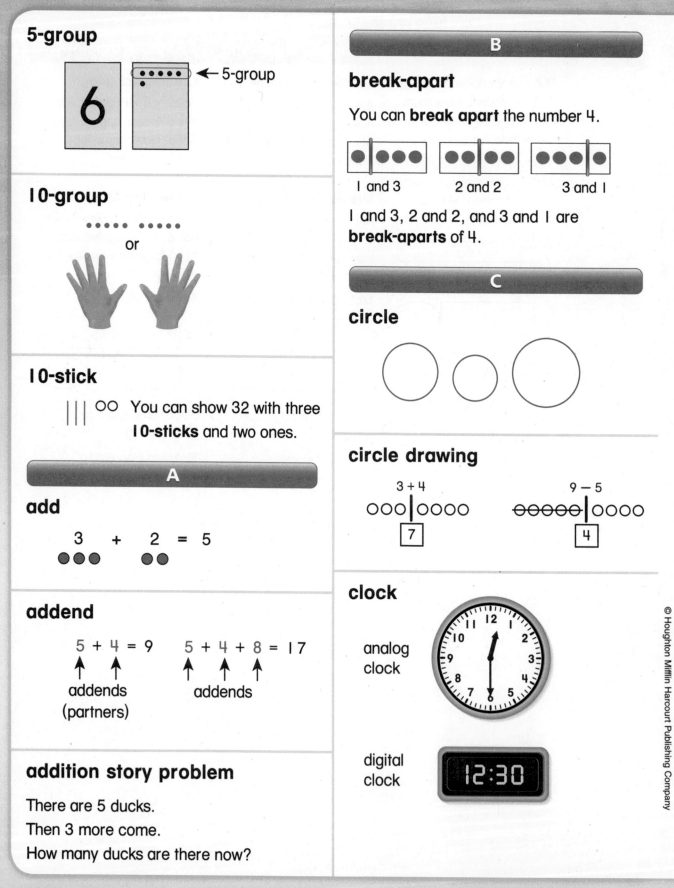

6 ← 5-group

10-group

• • • • •   • • • • •

or

10-stick

| | | ○○ You can show 32 with three **10-sticks** and two ones.

A

add

3 + 2 = 5
●●● ●●

addend

5 + 4 = 9   5 + 4 + 8 = 17
↑ ↑   ↑ ↑ ↑
addends   addends
(partners)

addition story problem

There are 5 ducks.
Then 3 more come.
How many ducks are there now?

B

break-apart

You can **break apart** the number 4.

| • | • • • | | • • | • • | | • • • | • |
1 and 3   2 and 2   3 and 1

1 and 3, 2 and 2, and 3 and 1 are
break-aparts of 4.

C

circle

circle drawing

3 + 4
○○○ | ○○○○
7

9 − 5
⊘⊘⊘⊘⊘ | ○○○○
4

clock

analog clock

digital clock

12:30

column

1	11	21	31	41	51	61	71	81	91
2	12	22	32	42	52	62	72	82	92
3	13	23	33	43	53	63	73	83	93
4	14	24	34	44	54	64	74	84	94
5	15	25	35	45	55	65	75	85	95
6	16	26	36	46	56	66	76	86	96
7	17	27	37	47	57	67	77	87	97
8	18	28	38	48	58	68	78	88	98
9	19	29	39	49	59	69	79	89	99
10	20	30	40	50	60	70	80	90	100

compare

You can **compare** numbers.

11 is less than 12.

$$11 < 12$$

12 is greater than 11.

$$12 > 11$$

You can **compare** objects by length.

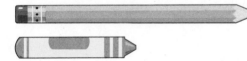

The crayon is shorter than the pencil.

The pencil is longer than the crayon.

comparison bars

Joe has 6 roses. Sasha has 9 roses. How many more roses does Sasha have than Joe?

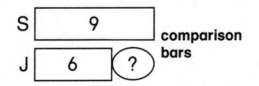

comparison bars

cone

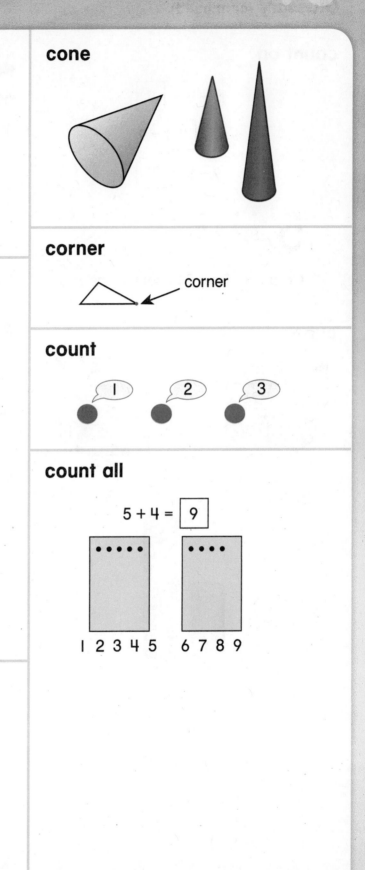

corner

corner

count

1 2 3

count all

$$5 + 4 = \boxed{9}$$

• • • • •   • • • •

1 2 3 4 5   6 7 8 9

count on

$$5 + 4 = \boxed{9}$$

$$5 + \boxed{4} = 9$$

$$9 - 5 = \boxed{4}$$

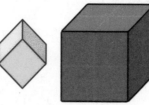

5 6 7 8 9

Count on from 5 to get the answer.

cube

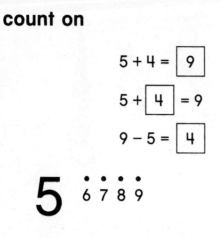

cylinder

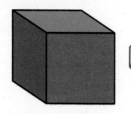

data

Colors in the Bag								
Red	○	○	○					
Yellow	○	○	○	○	○	○	○	○
Blue	○	○	○	○	○	○		

The **data** show how many of each color.

decade numbers

10, 20, 30, 40, 50, 60, 70, 80, 90

difference

$$11 - 3 = 8$$

$$\begin{array}{r} 11 \\ -\ 3 \\ \hline 8 \end{array}$$

difference →

digit

15 is a 2-**digit** number.

The 1 in 15 means 1 ten.

The 5 in 15 means 5 ones.

Dot Array

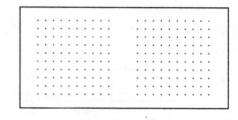

doubles

$$4 + 4 = 8$$

Both partners are the same.
They are **doubles**.

doubles minus 1

$7 + 7 = 14$, so

$7 + 6 = 13$, 1 less than 14.

doubles minus 2

$7 + 7 = 14$, so

$7 + 5 = 12$, 2 less than 14.

doubles plus 1

$6 + 6 = 12$, so

$6 + 7 = 13$, 1 more than 12.

doubles plus 2

$6 + 6 = 12$, so

$6 + 8 = 14$, 2 more than 12.

E

edge

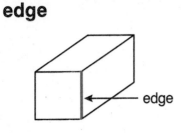

edge

equal shares

2 equal shares   4 equal shares

These show **equal shares**.

equal to (=)

$$4 + 4 = 8$$

4 plus 4 is **equal to** 8.

equation

Examples:

$4 + 3 = 7$ $7 = 4 + 3$

$9 - 5 = 4$ $4 = 9 - 5$

F

face

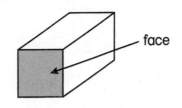

face

fewer

Eggs Laid This Month

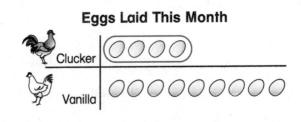

Clucker

Vanilla

Clucker laid **fewer** eggs than Vanilla.

fewest

Eggs Laid This Month

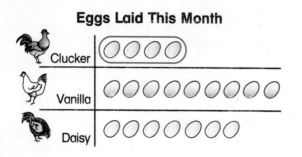

Clucker laid the **fewest** eggs.

fourth of

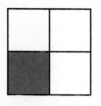

One **fourth of** the shape is shaded.

fourths

 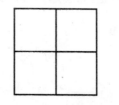

I whole   4 **fourths**, or 4 quarters

G

greater than (>)

34   >   25

34 is greater than 25.

grid

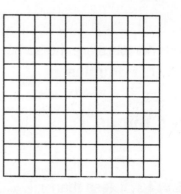

H

half-hour

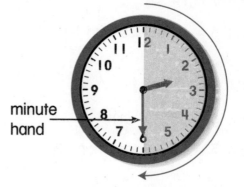

A **half-hour** is 30 minutes.

half of

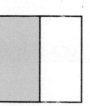

One **half of** the shape is shaded.

halves

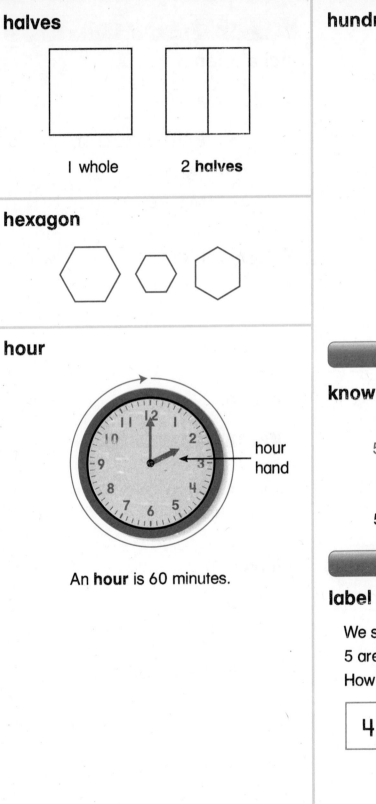

I whole   2 halves

hexagon

hour

An **hour** is 60 minutes.

hour hand

hundred

1	11	21	31	41	51	61	71	81	91
2	12	22	32	42	52	62	72	82	92
3	13	23	33	43	53	63	73	83	93
4	14	24	34	44	54	64	74	84	94
5	15	25	35	45	55	65	75	85	95
6	16	26	36	46	56	66	76	86	96
7	17	27	37	47	57	67	77	87	97
8	18	28	38	48	58	68	78	88	98
9	19	29	39	49	59	69	79	89	99
10	20	30	40	50	60	70	80	90	100

or

known partner

$5 + \boxed{} = 7$

5 is the **known partner**.

label

We see 9 fish.
5 are big. The others are small.
How many fish are small?

$\boxed{4}$ _____ fish

label

length

The **length** of this pencil is 6 paper clips.

less than (<)

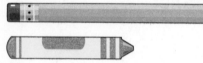

45   <   46

45 is less than 46.

longer

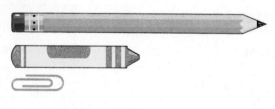

The pencil is **longer** than the crayon.

longest

The pencil is **longest**.

---

make a ten

$8 + 6 = \boxed{}$

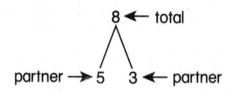

$10 + 4 = 14,$
so $8 + 6 = 14.$

Math Mountain

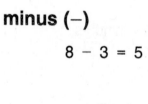

8 ← total

partner → 5   3 ← partner

measure

You can use paper clips to **measure** the length of the pencil.

minus (−)

$$8 - 3 = 5 \qquad \begin{array}{r} 8 \\ -3 \\ \hline 5 \end{array}$$

8 **minus** 3 equals 5.

minute

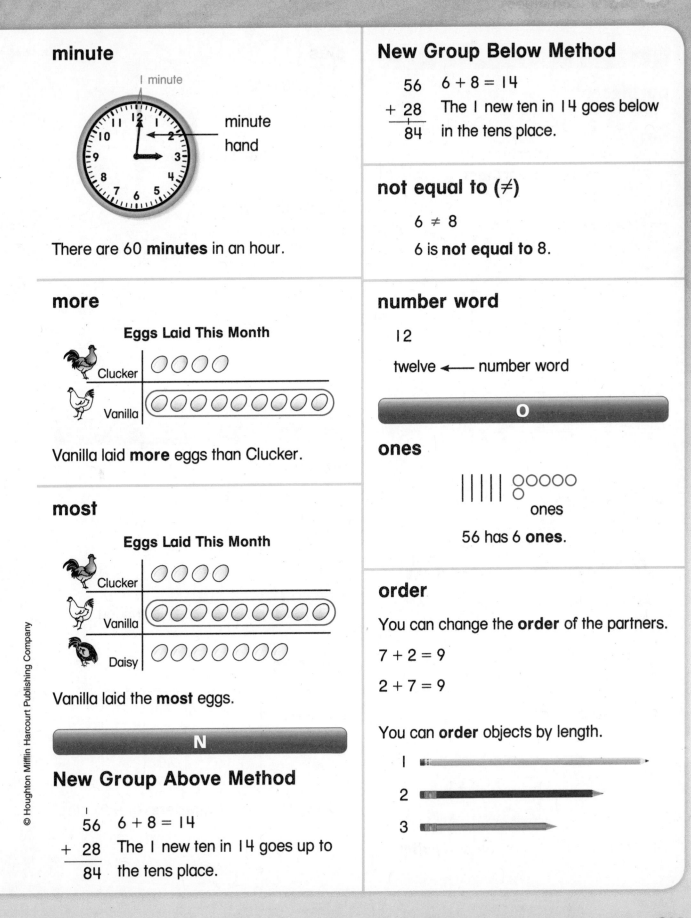

There are 60 **minutes** in an hour.

more

Eggs Laid This Month

Clucker

Vanilla

Vanilla laid **more** eggs than Clucker.

most

Eggs Laid This Month

Clucker

Vanilla

Daisy

Vanilla laid the **most** eggs.

N

New Group Above Method

$$\begin{array}{r} \overset{1}{56} \\ + 28 \\ \hline 84 \end{array}$$

$6 + 8 = 14$
The 1 new ten in 14 goes up to the tens place.

New Group Below Method

$$\begin{array}{r} 56 \\ + 28 \\ \hline 84 \end{array}$$

$6 + 8 = 14$
The 1 new ten in 14 goes below in the tens place.

not equal to (≠)

$6 \neq 8$

6 is **not equal to** 8.

number word

12

twelve ⟵ number word

O

ones

||||| ⭕⭕⭕⭕⭕
ones

56 has 6 **ones**.

order

You can change the **order** of the partners.

$7 + 2 = 9$

$2 + 7 = 9$

You can **order** objects by length.

1

2

3

© Houghton Mifflin Harcourt Publishing Company

P

partner

5 = 2 + 3

2 and 3 are **partners** of 5.
2 and 3 are 5-**partners**.

partner house

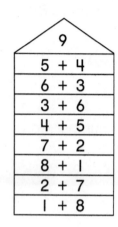

partner train

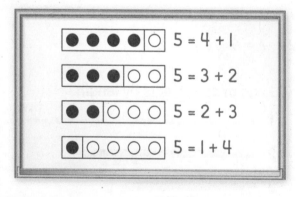

pattern

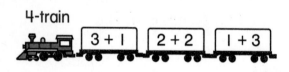

The partners of a number show a **pattern**.

plus (+)

3 + 2 = 5

$$\begin{array}{r} 3 \\ + 2 \\ \hline 5 \end{array}$$

3 **plus** 2 equals 5.

Proof Drawing

Q

quarter of

One **quarter of** the shape is shaded.

quarters

I whole   4 **quarters**, or 4 fourths

R

rectangle

A square is a special kind of rectangle.

rectangular prism

A cube is a special kind of rectangular prism.

row

1	11	21	31	41	51	61	71	81	91
2	12	22	32	42	52	62	72	82	92
3	13	23	33	43	53	63	73	83	93
4	14	24	34	44	54	64	74	84	94
5	15	25	35	45	55	65	75	85	95
6	16	26	36	46	56	66	76	86	96
7	17	27	37	47	57	67	77	87	97
8	18	28	38	48	58	68	78	88	98
9	19	29	39	49	59	69	79	89	99
10	20	30	40	50	60	70	80	90	100

S

shapes

2-dimensional   3-dimensional

shorter

The crayon is **shorter** than the pencil.

shortest

The paper clip is the **shortest**.

Show All Totals Method

$$
\begin{array}{r}
25 \\
+\ 48 \\
\hline
60 \\
13 \\
\hline
73
\end{array}
$$

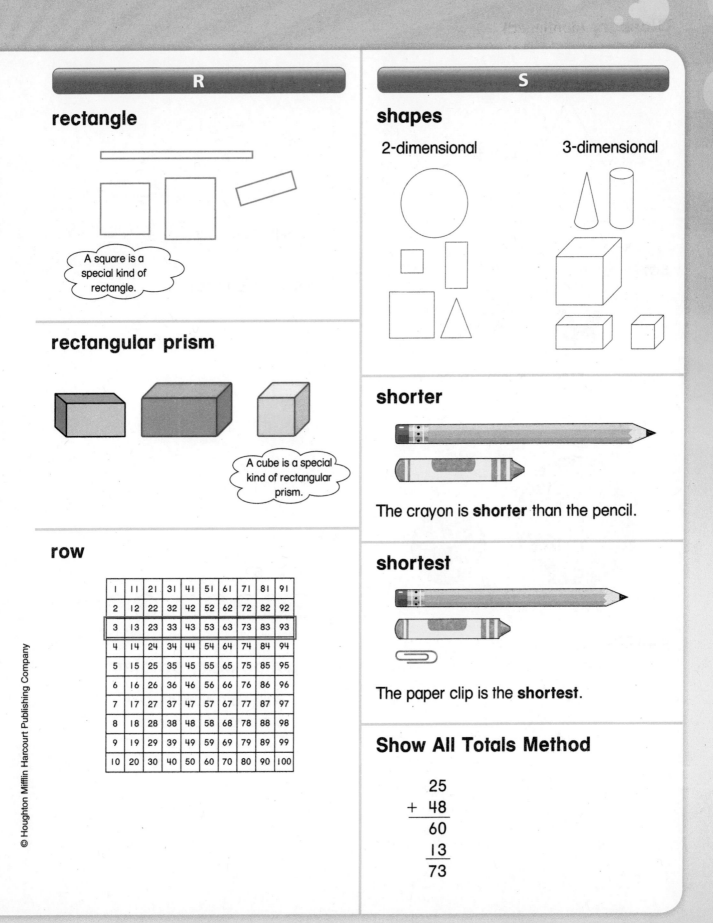

side

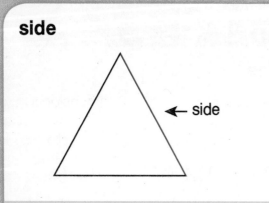

← side

sort

You can **sort** the bugs into groups.

sphere

square

square corner

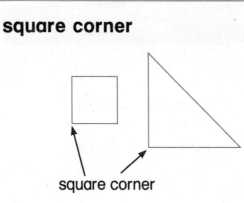

square corner

sticks and circles

I ○

II | ○

2I || ○

3I ||| ○

subtract

8 − 3 = 5

subtraction story problem

8 flies are on a log.
6 are eaten by a frog.
How many flies are left?

switch the partners

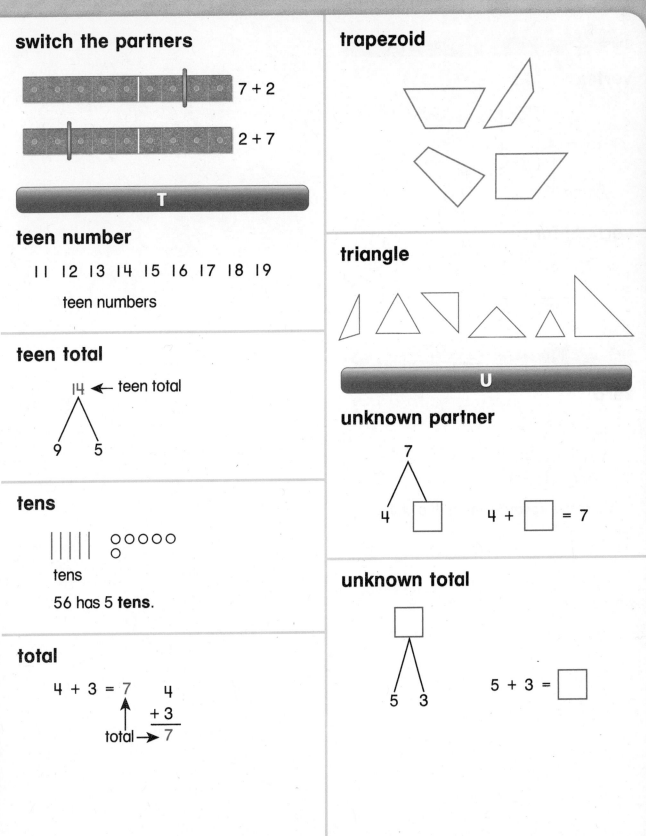

7 + 2

2 + 7

T

teen number

11 12 13 14 15 16 17 18 19

teen numbers

teen total

14 ← teen total

9   5

tens

tens

56 has 5 **tens**.

total

4 + 3 = 7

$$\begin{array}{r} 4 \\ + 3 \\ \hline 7 \end{array}$$

total →

trapezoid

triangle

U

unknown partner

7

4

4 + ☐ = 7

unknown total

5   3

5 + 3 = ☐

V

vertex

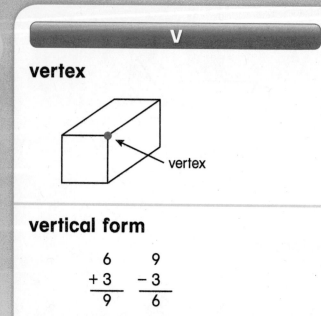

vertex

vertical form

$$
\begin{array}{r} 6 \\ +3 \\ \hline 9 \end{array}
\qquad
\begin{array}{r} 9 \\ -3 \\ \hline 6 \end{array}
$$

Z

zero

There are **zero** apples on the plate.